Basic Skills for the TOEFL® iBT

Iain Donald Binns
Micah Sedillos

Compass Publishing

D1534179

Listening 2

Basic Skills for the TOEFL® iBT 2

Listening

Iain Donald Binns · Micah Sedillos

© 2008 Compass Publishing

Project Editor: Liana Robinson
Acquisitions Editor: Emily Page
Content Editor: Erik Custer
Copy Editor: Alice Wrigglesworth
Contributing Writers: Kayang Gagiano, Edaan Getzel, Moraig Macgillivray
Consultants: Lucy Han, Chanhee Park
Cover/Interior Design: Dammora Inc.

email: info@compasspub.com
http://www.compasspub.com

ISBN: 978-1-59966-155-1

10 9 8 7 6 5 4 3
10 09

Photo Credits
pp. 24, 44, 54, 64, 74, 102, 112, 122, 148, 150 © Jupiterimages Corporation
pp. 34, 92, 132, 146 © iStock International Inc.
pp. 78, 80, 142 © Shutterstock, Inc.
pp. 82 © BigStockPhoto

Contents

Introduction to the TOEFL® iBT

What is the TOEFL® test?

The TOEFL® iBT test (Test of English as a Foreign Language Internet-based test) is designed to assess English proficiency in non-native speakers who want to achieve academic success as well as effective communication. It is not meant to test academic knowledge or computer ability; therefore, questions are always based on material found in the test.

The TOEFL® iBT test is divided into four sections:

- Reading
- Speaking
- Listening
- Writing

TOEFL® Scores

TOEFL® scores can be used for:

- Admission into university or college where instruction is in English
- Employers or government agencies who need to determine a person's English ability
- English-learning institutes who need to place students in the appropriate level of English instruction

It is estimated that about 4,400 universities and other institutions require a certain TOEFL® test score for admission.

The exact calculation of a TOEFL® test score is complicated and not necessary for the student to understand. However, it is helpful to know that:

- Each section in the Internet-based test is worth 30 points
- The highest possible score on the iBT is 120 points
- Each institution will have its own specific score requirements

✱ It is very important to check with each institution individually to find out what its admission requirements are.

Registering for the TOEFL® iBT

Students who wish to take the TOEFL® test must get registration information. Registration information can be obtained online at the ETS website. The Internet address is www.ets.org/toefl.

The website provides information such as:

- testing locations
- identification requirements
- registration information
- costs
- other test preparation material
- test center locations

This information will vary depending on the country in which you take the test. Be sure to follow the requirements carefully. If you do not have the proper requirements in order, you may not be able to take the test. Remember that if you register online, you will need to have your credit card information ready.

Introduction to the Listening Section of the TOEFL® iBT

In the listening section of the TOEFL® test, you will hear a variety of conversations and lectures, each of which lasts from 3–6 minutes. A total of six listening passages will be presented. After each passage, you will then be asked to answer 5–6 questions about what you heard. These questions are designed to test your ability to

- recognize and understand the main idea
- determine factual information
- determine inference

You will not be asked questions regarding vocabulary or sentence structure. You will not be permitted to see the questions until after you have listened to the conversation or lecture. Although some questions will replay part of the conversation or lecture, you cannot choose to listen to it again while answering the questions. You do not need any previous knowledge on the topic in order to answer the questions correctly.

Passage Types

1. Conversations—two people discussing a campus-related problem, issue, or process
2. Lectures—a professor speaking a monologue, presenting information related to an academic topic
3. Classroom interaction—similar to the lecture passage type, but with some interaction between the professor and one or more students

Listening Question Types

Most questions will be normal multiple-choice. However, the other types are

- multiple-choice questions with more than one answer
- replay questions where the test taker will listen to part of the conversation again before choosing the correct answer
- questions that asks the test taker to put events or steps of a process in order
- questions that require the test taker to match text or objects to a category

The following list explains the types and number of each question per listening passage on the TOEFL® iBT test. Questions may not always appear in this order.

Question Type	Number	Description
Main Idea	1	Choose the best phrase or sentence
Detail	1–2	Choose the statement that is true according to the listening passage
Function	1–2	Choose the answer that explains why the speaker has said something
Attitude	1–2	Choose the answer that describes the speaker's emotion, attitude, or opinion
Organization	0–1	Explain how or why the speaker communicated certain information
Content	0–1	Select the answers that feature points from the listening passage

Most questions are worth 1 point each; however, some may be worth more.

Test management:

- A visual image will be given on the screen to allow test takers to recognize each speaker's role and the context of the conversation.
- Before you begin the listening section, listen to the headset directions. Pay particular attention to how you change the volume. It is very important that you be able to hear clearly during the listening section of the test.
- If you miss something that is said in a conversation or lecture, do not panic. Forget about it, and simply keep listening. Even native speakers do not hear everything that is said.
- Note-taking during the lecture is permitted. Paper will be provided by the test supervisor. These notes can be studied while answering the questions.
- Like the reading section, questions cannot be viewed until after the lecture/conversation has been completed.
- You must answer each question as it appears. You can NOT return to any questions later.
- Do not leave any questions unanswered. You are NOT penalized for guessing an answer.

Introduction to the *Basic Skills for the TOEFL® iBT* series

Basic Skills for the TOEFL® iBT is a 3-level, 12-book test preparation series designed for beginning-level students of the TOEFL® iBT. Over the course of the series, students build on their current vocabulary to include common TOEFL® and academic vocabulary. They are also introduced to the innovative questions types found in the TOEFL® iBT, and are provided with practice of TOEFL® iBT reading, listening, speaking, and writing passages, conversations, lectures, and questions accessible to students of their level.

Basic Skills for the TOEFL® iBT enables students to build on both their language skills and their knowledge. The themes of the passages, lectures, and questions cover the topics often seen on the TOEFL® iBT. In addition, the independent topics, while taking place in a university setting, are also accessible to and understood by students preparing to enter university. The academic topics are also ones that native speakers study.

Students accumulate vocabulary over the series. Vocabulary learned at the beginning of the series will appear in passages and lectures later in the book, level, and series. Each level gets progressively harder. The vocabulary becomes more difficult, the number of vocabulary words to be learned increases, and the passages, conversations, and lectures get longer and increase in level. By the end of the series, students will know all 570 words on the standard Academic Word List (AWL) used by TESOL and have a solid foundation in and understanding of the TOEFL® iBT.

Not only will *Basic Skills for the TOEFL® iBT* start preparing students for the TOEFL® iBT, but it will also give students a well-rounded basis for either further academic study in English or further TOEFL® iBT study.

Introduction to the *Basic Skills for the TOEFL® iBT* Listening Book

This is the second listening book in the *Basic Skills for the TOEFL® iBT* series. The student will listen to two conversations and two lectures in each unit. The conversations will be between either a student and a university employee or a student and a professor. The lectures will be on the topics that the student was introduced to in the Level 2 reading book. The conversations and lectures in *Listening Level 2* are longer and at a higher level, the questions are slightly more difficult, and there are more vocabulary words compared to *Listening Level 1*.

Each unit is separated into seven sections:

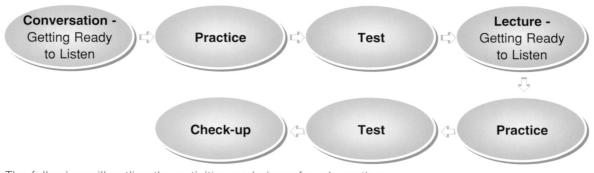

The following will outline the activities and aims of each section.

Conversation - Getting Ready to Listen

Key Vocabulary and TOEFL Vocabulary

Students begin by studying the vocabulary they will encounter in the following conversation. **TOEFL® Vocabulary** is the words that have been found to appear most often in TOEFL® preparation materials or are Academic Word List (AWL) words. TOEFL® Vocabulary are the most important words for the student to learn in order to build their vocabulary before further TOEFL® study. **Key Vocabulary** are the other words that are important for the student to know in order to understand the conversation that will follow.

TOEFL Question Types

In this part, students will become familiar with
- one of the question types that appear in the TOEFL® iBT listening section
- the common wording of this question type in the conversation section
- the aims of the question type
- the strategy for correctly answering the question

Becoming familiar with the question types and how to answer them is important for the student, as it will help them answer the questions appropriately. Level 2 builds on the strategies the student learned in level 1.

Over the course of the book, all the listening question types will be covered.

Practice

Conversation

Students listen to the first part of the first conversation. They then answer two multiple-choice questions, which help the student to identify the main idea and purpose of the conversation. Listening to only the first part of the conversation enables the students to practice listening for main ideas without having to focus on the details.

Note-taking

Students now listen to the full conversation. It contains the vocabulary words learned on the previous page, so there should be very few words that the student is unfamiliar with. Although the conversation is based in a university, it is accessible to and understood by students preparing to enter university. This helps students become used to listening to university-situated conversations but at a level they can understand.

Students take notes as they listen to the conversation. The notes are guided so that the student only has to fill in the parts that are missing. This introduces the students to a common way of conversation note-taking. This enables them to become used to thinking about not only the passage in general but also specific details and how the main idea is developed throughout the conversation.

TOEFL Questions

The next page gives students the opportunity to practice the question types they were introduced to in this unit and the previous unit. There will be two of the question type learned in this unit and one from the previous unit. They will be worded in the same way as they are in the real TOEFL® test.

TOEFL Vocabulary Practice

The next part is sentences using the TOEFL® vocabulary the student learned at the beginning of the section. This helps students practice the words in context.

Test

The test contains the second conversation of the unit. It is similar to the real TOEFL® test, but at an appropriate level for the student. It gives the student the opportunity to practice many question types at the same time. The test passage also uses many of the vocabulary words learned at the beginning of the section.

Lecture - Getting Ready to Listen

Key Vocabulary and TOEFL Vocabulary

This is the Key Vocabulary and TOEFL® Vocabulary they will encounter in following lecture. See the conversation description for further details.

TOEFL Question Type

In this part, students will become familiar with
- one of the question types that appear in the TOEFL® iBT Listening section
- the common wording of this question type in the lecture section
- the aims of the question type
- the strategy for correctly answering the question

See the conversation description for further details.

Practice

Lecture

Students listen to the first part of the first lecture. They then answer three multiple-choice questions, which help the student to identify the main idea, purpose, and organization of the lecture. The fourth multiple-choice question asks the student to identify the best note-taking diagram to use for the lecture. Students can look at the answers to the previous three multiple-choice questions to help them decide. Listening to only the first part of the lecture enables the students to practice listening for main ideas and structure without having to focus on the details.

Note-taking

Students now draw the note-taking diagram they chose in the previous question. They can then insert the information from questions 1 and 2. They will then listen to the full lecture and fill in the rest of the notes. The lecture contains the vocabulary words learned on the previous page, so there should be very few words that the student is unfamiliar with.

Using the designated note-taking diagram introduces the students to a common way of note-taking for the type of lecture. This enables them to become used to different ways to take notes and how to identify the lecture's specific details and how its main idea is developed and organized.

TOEFL Questions

The next page gives students the opportunity to practice the question types they were introduced to in this unit and the previous unit. There will be two of the question type learned in this unit and one from the previous unit. They will be worded in the same way as they are in the real TOEFL® test.

TOEFL Vocabulary Practice

The next part is sentences using the TOEFL® vocabulary learned at the beginning of the lecture section. This helps students practice the words in context.

Test

The test contains the second lecture of the unit. It is longer than the first lecture, but it will build on its content. This test is similar to the real TOEFL® test, but at an appropriate level for the student. It gives the student the opportunity to practice many question types at the same time. The test passage also uses many of the vocabulary words learned at the beginning of the lecture section.

Check-up

Question Type Review

These questions check the student understands the question type that was focused on throughout the unit.

Key Vocabulary Practice

This part is sentences using the Key vocabulary the student learned over the course of the unit. This helps students practice the words in context.

Introduction to Note-taking Diagrams for Listening Lectures

The note-taking diagrams shown below are used throughout the book. This explains the diagrams a little further.

Units 1 and 7
Concept Defining Diagram

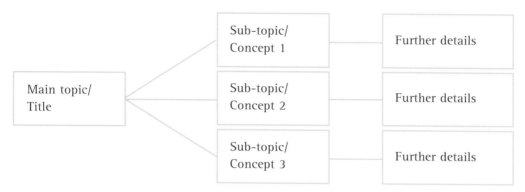

This note-taking diagram is used to define the concepts of an overall topic. There can be many or only a few boxes coming off the main topic. There may also be another level that contains further details. In this book, there will only be a few subtopics/concepts and a few further details.

Units 2 and 8
Venn Diagram

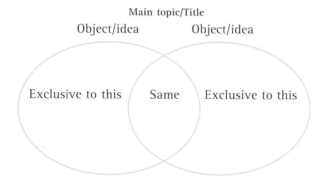

This note-taking diagram is used to compare and contrast objects and ideas. They are usually related under a common heading. There can be two or three circles. In this book, there will only be two things compared, thus only two circles will be needed.

Units 3 and 9
Problem and Solution Diagram

Problem	Solution
(Overall problem)	(Overall solution)

• Problem   →
  - further details
• Problem   →
  - further details
• Problem   →
  - further details
	• Solution
	  - further details
	• Solution
	  - further details
	• Solution
	  - further details

This note-taking diagram is used to show problems and their solutions. There may be many problems with many solutions or there may be one overall problem that has different solutions. In this book, there will only be a few problems with up to a couple of solutions each.

Units 4 and 10
Categorizing Diagram

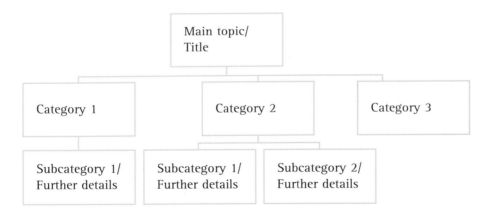

This note-taking diagram is used to show problems and their solutions. There may be many problems with many solutions or there may be one overall problem that is experienced by many things and therefore has different solutions. In this book, there will only be a few problems with up to a couple of solutions each.

Units 5 and 11
Ordering Diagram

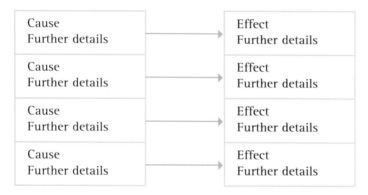

This note-taking diagram is used to show the sequence of events or steps in a process. There can be many or only a few boxes and many or only a few details about each step. In this book, there will only be a few steps with each containing only a few further details.

Units 6 and 12
Cause and Effect Diagram

Main Topic/Title

Cause Further details	Effect Further details
Cause Further details	Effect Further details
Cause Further details	Effect Further details
Cause Further details	Effect Further details

This note-taking diagram is used to show what happens when something changes or is created. Each cause and effect can be completely independent from, or related to, the one above or below it. There can be many or only a few cause and effects with many or only a few details about each. In this book, there will be either many boxes with few details, or a few boxes with many details.

Sample Listening Lesson Plan - 50 minutes

Homework Check	5 min.	• Talk about any homework questions that the students did not understand. A combination of both teacher and peer explanations should be used.
Review	5 min.	• Review the strategies discussed in the previous lesson and talk about other strategies students might have employed when they did homework.
Main Lesson	35 min.	✳ Students often find conversations easier, so they should complete it for homework. The conversations and lectures could also be alternately taught in the classroom. **Lecture - Getting Ready to Listen** A. Learn the words • Preview the vocabulary and have students read the words aloud. • Talk about what parts of speech the words belong to. ✳ Vocabulary preview can also be done immediately before the first lecture. B. Learn the question type • Discuss how the wording of the lecture version of the question type differs from the conversation version. (The strategies for the question type should have been learned at the end of the previous lesson and reviewed at the beginning) **Practice** A. Lecture • Ask the students to listen to the first part of the lecture and answer the first three questions either on their own or with a partner. • Talk about the main points and the organization of the passage as a class. • Do the fourth question as a class and explain why the note-taking diagram is most appropriate and how to use it. B and C. Note-taking • Have students draw the diagram and fill in some of the notes. Then check as a class that students have filled in the first part of the notes in the same way. • Have students listen to the rest of the lecture and fill in the rest of the notes. • Ask students to compare their notes with a classmate. • Emphasize that each student's notes may be written differently but that they should all include the same points. D. TOEFL Questions • Ask students to do the questions. Then, as a class or in pairs, talk about the strategies they used to answer the questions. • In pairs or by themselves, ask the students to make another question, using the target question type. When finished, have the students ask their classmates their question. E. TOEFL Vocabulary Practice • Ask students to complete the sentences and check their answers in pairs. **Test** • Students should complete the test individually. • Compare notes and discuss as a class what strategies were used. **Conversation - Getting Ready to Listen** (Next unit) A. Learn the words • Preview the vocabulary and have students read the words aloud • Talk about what parts of speech the words belong to. B. Learn the Question Type • Introduce the TOEFL® question type. • Discuss strategies that can be applied to the question type.
Wrap-up	5 min.	• Give homework (the rest of the conversation section.) ✳ The lecture test section and check-up section can also be given as homework.

Teaching Tips

- It is strongly recommended to go through the target vocabulary prior to listening.

- It is a good idea to have students make their own vocabulary list on their PC or notebook. Putting the words under thematic categories (categories of subjects) would be an effective way to study the words.

- It is important to emphasize understanding of the main idea of the conversations and lectures. Students often listen without constructing the framework, which could cause problems understanding the main points later.

- It is important to emphasize understanding of the organization of the lectures. Understanding this enables students to choose the most appropriate note-taking diagram for the type of lecture.

- The first class should take time to introduce the note-taking diagrams. Then when students are asked to use the diagrams, they are familiar and, therefore, not as intimidating.

- In the beginning, note-taking practice needs to be done in class with the teacher's assistance because not many students are familiar with note-taking. Gradually, have students take notes in groups, pairs, and then individually.

- At least one lecture and the following questions should be done as an in-class activity; otherwise, students will not be able to understand the strategies and the new information.

- Timed question taking is an effective activity. Teachers can change the time limit as students' understanding increases.

- Encourage students to do timed activities even when they do their homework. It is a good idea to record the time they take to do the tests in their book and how many times they replayed the listening passages.

- Written and oral summaries of the lectures and conversations are recommended in order to help students understand the main point, the overall meaning, and the structure. It is also a useful exercise to prepare for the speaking and writing sections.

- Students can use the definitions and synonyms in the vocabulary section when they summarize or paraphrase the passages.

- Use the test at the end of each unit as a progress check by recording the scores of the tests, the time taken to complete the test, and the number of times the listening passage was replayed.

[01] Conversation

Getting Ready to Listen

A. Learn the words.

Key Vocabulary

student center	a central public meeting place for students at a university
auditorium	a building commonly used for events such as concerts or lectures
hang out	to spend time together
supplies	things, such as pencils and pens, used to accomplish a task

TOEFL Vocabulary

assistance	aid; help
recreation	an activity that a person takes part in for pleasure
discount	a reduced price
collect	to obtain
verify	to confirm

B. Learn the question type.

TOEFL Question Type

Main Idea

What are the speakers mainly discussing?

Why does the student visit the professor/librarian/etc?

Why does the professor ask to see the student?

- "Why" main idea questions are more commonly asked regarding conversations.
- Refer to your notes and look for the main problem the student is trying to solve.

Practice

A. Listen to the first part of the conversation and choose the correct answers.

Track 1-1

1. What is the main topic of this conversation?

(A) The student needs help finding the student center.

(B) The student wants to purchase school supplies.

2. How does the woman explain where the student center is?

(A) She tells him to go find a map in the library.

(B) She shows it to him and gives him directions how to get there.

Note-taking

B. Listen to the full conversation and take notes. Track 1-2

Man - Student	Woman - Student Guide
• Can't find _____ _____ _____ _____ _____ _____ _____ _____ _____ _____	• It is next to the _____ _____ • The bookstore, cafeteria, _____ _____ • You can buy _____ _____ _____ _____ _____ _____ _____

C. Choose the correct answers.

1. What problem does the man have?

    (A) He is unable to find the library.

    (B) He needs help to find the student center.

2. What is the conversation mainly about?

    (A) An in-depth description on how to get a new student ID

    (B) A brief explanation of where the student center is located and what is in it

3. According to the woman, which of the following is true?

    (A) Offices, like the student newspaper and recreation office, are located in the student center.

    (B) You can find out about concerts at the student center but you have to purchase the tickets at the auditorium.

TOEFL Vocabulary Practice

D. Fill in the blanks with the correct words.

assistance	recreation	discount	collect	verify

1. New students often need _____ finding their classes.

2. The office attendant needs to see the employee's ID to _____ their identity.

3. For _____, married couples might like to go hiking.

4. University students are often offered a(n) _____ when purchasing tickets.

5. The winner can _____ his or her prize at the door.

Test

Listen to the conversation and take notes. **Track 1-3**

Man - University Employee	Woman - Student
• The tickets are different _____ _____ _____ • Student ticket $10, _____	• Wants to buy tickets for _____ _____ • Would like to buy one ticket for _____

Choose the correct answers. **Track 1-4**

1. Why is the woman talking to the university employee?

(A) She is interested in purchasing concert tickets.
(B) She needs help locating the student center.
(C) She is interested in joining a school club.
(D) She needs to make a payment of his tuition.

2. Why would the student need to take his ID with her?

(A) To get it scanned to pay for her lunch
(B) To get the tickets replaced
(C) To verify that she is the person who bought the tickets
(D) To verify that she is a freshman in college

3. What is the attitude of the student buying the tickets?

(A) She feels the prices are unreasonable.
(B) She thinks the employee is being unfair.
(C) She is happy with the ticket prices.
(D) She wants a bigger discount.

4. Indicate which of the following is mentioned in the conversation.

(A) University students receive free tickets.
(B) University students receive discounts.
(C) University students always pay five dollars less.
(D) Non-students have free entrance into the concert.

Lecture - History

Getting Ready to Listen

A. Learn the words.

Key Vocabulary

pyramid	a large structure with a square base and triangular sides which meet at the top
quarry	a large pit in the earth where stone is mined
pharaoh	an Egyptian king
afterlife	a life people believe they will have after death

TOEFL Vocabulary

structure	something that has been built
historian	a person who studies history
ancient	very old
committed	dedicated
furthermore	in addition

B. Learn the question type.

TOEFL Question Type

Main Idea

What aspect of X does the professor mainly discuss?

What is the lecture mainly about?

- The answer will be the choice that best reflects what the professor's aim is (e.g., introduce a new topic, expand on a previously discussed issue) or what he or she is mainly talking about.
- Refer to your notes and look for repeated content words or phrases.

Practice

A. **Listen to the first part of the lecture and choose the correct answers.** `Track 1-5`

1. What is the main topic of this lecture?
   (A) Egyptian pharaohs   (B) Egyptian pyramids

2. What are the key points of the lecture?
   (A) Where the pyramids and the pharaohs are found
   (B) What materials were used, how the pyramids were built, and the purpose of them

3. How does the professor describe the main topic?
   (A) By giving examples   (B) By comparing and contrasting

4. Choose the best note-taking diagram for this lecture.

   (A) Venn Diagram   (B) Concept Defining   (C) Problem and Solution
                             Diagram   Diagram

Note-taking

B. **Draw the diagram chosen in question 4. Then insert the information from questions 1 and 2.**

C. **Now listen to the full lecture and complete your notes.** `Track 1-6`

D. Choose the correct answers.

1. What is the lecture mainly about?

    (A) How the pyramids were built

    (B) What the pyramids were made of

2. What is the main idea of the lecture?

    (A) There is some mystery as to when the pyramids were built.

    (B) There is some mystery as to how the pyramids were built.

3. According to the lecture, why was gold placed in the pyramids?

    (A) Because the pharaohs thought they would need it in the afterlife

    (B) So that no one could steal it

TOEFL Vocabulary Practice

E. Fill in the blanks with the correct words.

structure	historians	ancient	committed	furthermore

1. To get a good job, you need credentials and experience. _____, it helps to have good references.

2. The best employees are ones who are _____ to their jobs.

3. The Great Wall of China is said to be the largest man-made _____ in the world.

4. People who are interested in studying the past become _____.

5. Ruins give us information about _____ times.

Test

Listen to the lecture and take notes. Track 1-7

Evidence That Slaves Did Not Build the Pyramids

- Food

- Workers

- Graffiti

- The builders ate bread and meat

- Some were highly skilled and stayed all year

- Does not support idea they were slaves

Choose the correct answers. Track 1-8

1. What is the main idea of the lecture?

(A) The pyramids were not built by slaves.

(B) The slaves who build the pyramids were fed well.

(C) The pyramid builders worked for free.

(D) The pyramids were built by bakers and farmers.

2. When did the farmers work on the pyramids?

(A) Spring

(B) Summer

(C) Fall

(D) Winter

3. What is the professor's opinion as to who built the pyramids?

    (A) She thinks they were built only by slaves.

    (B) She thinks they were built only by farmers.

    (C) She thinks they were built by professional pyramid builders.

    (D) She thinks they were built by different types of seasonal workers.

4. Why does the professor mention graffiti?

    (A) As evidence that the pyramids were built by slaves

    (B) As evidence of the art found in the pyramid

    (C) As evidence that workers were unhappy

    (D) As evidence that workers were happy

5. Listen again to part of the lecture. Then answer the question. 🎧

    Why does the professor say this: 🎧 ?

    (A) To criticize pharaohs for keeping the best meat for themselves

    (B) To criticize pharaohs for mistreating slaves

    (C) To provide evidence that the slaves were well treated

    (D) To provide evidence that workers were not slaves

6. In the lecture, the professor describes evidence regarding who built the pyramids. Indicate whether each of the following is mentioned.

	YES	NO
Workers ate the best cuts of meat.		
Farmers helped work on the pyramids in the summer.		
The flooding of the Nile slowed down pyramid construction.		
Teenagers today ruined the pyramids with graffiti.		

Check-up

A. Choose the correct answers.

1. When answering a conversation main idea question
   (A) look at your notes for any pattern to how the points are presented, such as chronologically or by importance
   (B) refer to your notes for the central problem the student wants to solve
   (C) pay attention to the words and phrases spoken just before and after a repeated comment
   (D) look in your notes for any rhetorical questions asked by the speakers

2. What should you do when answering a lecture main idea question?
   (A) Choose the answer that best explains the idioms and expressions used in the lecture.
   (B) Look for the answer that best explains the speaker's tone of voice.
   (C) Choose the answer that puts the steps of a sequence into the correct order.
   (D) Look in your notes for repeated content words or phrases to give you a clue about the main idea.

Key Vocabulary Practice

B. Fill in the blanks with the correct words.

pyramids	quarry	pharaoh	afterlife
supplies	auditorium	student center	hang out

1. Different cultures have different beliefs about the _____.

2. Students often meet in the _____ for lunch.

3. After studying, students often like to _____ together and eat dinner.

4. Marble is mined from a(n) _____.

5. Many people go to Egypt to see the _____.

6. Drama students often practice a play in a(n) _____.

7. King Tutankhamen was an Egyptian _____.

8. For painting class, a professor has to buy art _____ for his or her students.

[02] Conversation

Getting Ready to Listen

A. Learn the words.

Key Vocabulary

resident assistant	a supervisor in a college dormitory, usually an upper classman; also shortened to RA
refund	a reimbursement of money, usually because of overpayment or from money that went unused
mistake	an incorrect decision, or a misunderstanding of something
payment	a certain amount of money paid toward something

TOEFL Vocabulary

accommodation	a place to live or stay
apparently	what seems to be the case but may not be
orientation	an event or meeting designed to introduce a place or program
presume	to assume that something is true
burden	a stressful responsibility

B. Learn the question type.

TOEFL Question Type

Detail

According to the man/woman, what is the main problem with X?

What does the man suggest the woman do?

- Refer to your notes for important details; the test will not ask for minor details.
- Select the answer choice most consistent with the speaker's relationship to the main problem of the conversation.

Practice

A. **Listen to the first part of the conversation and choose the correct answers.**

Track 1-9

1. What is the main topic of this conversation?

    (A) Receiving a refund on overpayment of tuition

    (B) A mistake made on a student's housing bill

2. How does the RA solve this problem?

    (A) Directs the student to go to the Office of Accommodation

    (B) Tells the student he needs to speak with his parents about payment

Note-taking

B. **Listen to the full conversation and take notes.** Track 1-10

Woman - Student	Man - RA
• Needs help with _____ _____ • Thinks she should be due _____ _____	• Directs her to the Office of _____ _____ • Tells her to take _____

C. Choose the correct answers.

1. What problem does the student have?

(A) She lost her wallet.

(B) She received a bill that is a mistake.

2. According to the RA, what does the student need to do to take care of her housing bill?

(A) Go to the Dean of Housing and tell him the bill is a mistake

(B) Go to the Office of Accommodation and they will be able to answer questions

3. According to the student, which of the following is true?

(A) She never paid her tuition.

(B) She paid her accommodation bill; in fact, she thinks she paid too much.

TOEFL Vocabulary Practice

D. Fill in the blanks with the correct words.

accommodation	apparently	orientation	presume	burden

1. When _____ is provided, students don't have to worry about housing.

2. Each student has the right to _____ the university is processing their information correctly.

3. _____, a meteor killed all the dinosaurs.

4. New employees at a cafeteria have to go to _____, in order to receive proper training.

5. No student wants his or her tuition to be a(n) _____.

Test

🎧 Listen to the conversation and take notes. `Track 1-11`

Man - Student	Woman - RA
• Moving out _____ _____ _____ _____ _____ _____ _____ _____	• Heard he is _____ • Might receive _____ _____ _____ _____ _____ _____

Choose the correct answers. `Track 1-12`

1. What is the conversation mainly about?

   (A) The student moving out of the dorm
   (B) The student wanting different roommates
   (C) The RA wanting the student to pay his housing fees
   (D) The Accommodation Office

2. According to the RA, what kind of refund will the student receive?

   (A) A full refund   (B) A partial refund
   (C) No refund   (D) None of the above

3. What does the RA imply when she says this: 🎧?

   (A) She hates his brother.
   (B) She thinks living with a brother can be difficult.
   (C) She doesn't know if her brother has space in his home.
   (D) Her brother lives in a different place.

4. Why does the RA discuss the Accommodation Office?

   (A) To tell the student about his job
   (B) To tell the student where he will be able to get some of his money back
   (C) To give an example of where to take care of financial needs
   (D) Because she had no other options to give the student

Lecture - Architecture

Getting Ready to Listen

A. Learn the words.

Key Vocabulary

prairie	a geographical region with flat land
dominant	most obvious
stand out	to be noticeable
floor plan	a design for the inside of a building

TOEFL Vocabulary

architectural	related to the design of buildings
several	being more than two but fewer than many
horizontal	side to side, as opposed to up and down
carve	to cut out of a material
contrary	in opposition to

B. Learn the question type.

TOEFL Question Type

Detail

According to the professor, what is one way that X can affect Y?
What resulted from X?

- The correct answer will usually be consistent with the main idea/topic of the lecture.
- Refer to your notes and look for key words written under main idea headings.

Practice

A. **Listen to the first part of the lecture and choose the correct answers.** `Track 1-13`

1. What is the main topic of the lecture?

   (A) The prairie landscape   (B) architectural styles

2. What are the key points in this lecture?

   (A) The prairies style differed from older styles because of lines and open plans.
   (B) Prairie-style homes were the same as older style homes, except they were built on prairies.

3. How does the professor describe the main topic?

   (A) By comparing and contrasting Wright's homes to previous ones
   (B) By outlining Wright's career and how his designs changed over time

4. Choose the best note-taking diagram for this lecture.

   (A) Problem and Solution   (B) Venn Diagram   (C) Ordering Diagram
   Diagram

Note-taking

B. **Draw the diagram chosen in question 4. Then insert the information from questions 1 and 2.**

C. **Now listen to the full lecture and complete your notes.** `Track 1-14`

32 | Listening |

D. Choose the correct answers.

1. What is the lecture mainly about?

   (A) The controversy surrounding Wright's designs

   (B) The new way Wright designed houses

2. What was named as a dominant feature of Wright's houses?

   (A) Vertical lines   (B) Horizontal lines

3. According to the professor, why did Wright's houses suit families in America during Wright's era?

   (A) More people were living in the prairies.

   (B) Parents wanted to be with their children more.

TOEFL Vocabulary Practice

E. Fill in the blanks with the correct words.

architectural	several	horizontal	carve	contrary

1. The top of a table is _____.

2. If there are more than two but less than ten, there are _____.

3. Some artists _____ sculptures out of wood.

4. People who want to design houses must take a(n) _____ course.

5. A teenager's behavior is often _____ to his or her parent's wishes.

Test

🎧 Listen to the lecture and take notes. **Track 1-15**

Architecture of John Lloyd Wright

- Dominant horizontal
- Hilly landscapes
- Separate rooms
- Solid corners
- Separate windows

Architectural Styles

Frank Lloyd Wright John Lloyd Wright

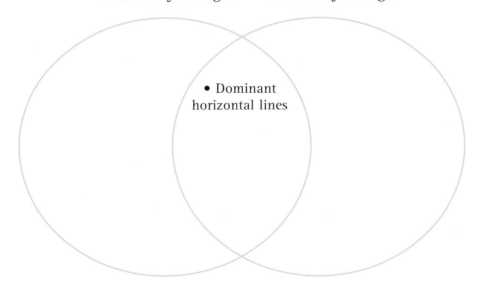

- Dominant horizontal lines

Choose the correct answers. **Track 1-16**

1. What is the lecture mainly about?

    (A) How John Lloyd Wright followed in his father's footsteps

    (B) How John Lloyd Wright rebelled against his father's wishes

    (C) How John Lloyd Wright created his own style of architecture

    (D) How John Lloyd Wright tried to imitate his father

2. Why does the professor mention Frank Lloyd Wright?

(A) To show how John Lloyd Wright got his start in architecture
(B) To give an example of a good teacher who produced a poor student
(C) To contrast John's architecture with the standard of the day
(D) To introduce the topic of the challenges faced by John Lloyd Wright

3. Which of the following is a feature that both John and Frank Lloyd Wright utilized?

(A) Open-concept floor plan
(B) Solid corners
(C) Connected windows
(D) Dominant horizontal lines

4. What is the professor's opinion of John Lloyd Wright?

(A) He thinks he revolutionized architecture in the US.
(B) He thinks he copied his father's work.
(C) He thinks he would not have been successful if it weren't for his father.
(D) He thinks he did a good job of creating his own style.

5. Why does the professor say this: ⌒ ?

(A) To suggest that being a famous architect's son has disadvantages
(B) To emphasize the difficulties faced by young architects starting out
(C) To suggest that Frank Lloyd Wright put a lot of pressure on his son
(D) To emphasize how hard one must work to become an architect

6. According to the professor, what is the likely outcome of using solid corners?

(A) Rooms will appear separate and distinct.
(B) Rooms will seem to flow into one another.
(C) Houses will blend in with surroundings.
(D) Houses will stand out against surroundings.

Check-up

A. Choose the correct answers.

1. When answering a conversation detail question
   (A) pick the answer that best describes the speaker's main problem
   (B) choose the answer that best explains the speaker's opinion
   (C) pick the answer most consistent with the speaker's relationship to the main problem
   (D) choose the answer that best summarizes the order of points made

2. What should you do when answering a lecture detail question?
   (A) Refer to your notes for key words under headings that support the main idea.
   (B) Refer to your notes for any rhetorical questions asked by the professor.
   (C) Select the answer that includes information that can be inferred from the professor's attitude.
   (D) Select the answer that explains why the professor tells a certain story during the lecture.

Key Vocabulary Practice

B. Fill in the blanks with the correct words.

prairies	RA	dominant	refunded
stand out	floor plan	payment	mistakes

1. Orange and yellow are _____ colors in autumn.

2. The parents made a(n) _____ on their child's first car.

3. The _____ are good for farming because there are no hills.

4. A(n) _____ is in charge of making sure all the students in the dorm are in their rooms by midnight.

5. Some animals use camouflage so they don't _____.

6. After completing the exam, students often realize the _____ they made.

7. The _____ shows how the rooms will be arranged in the house.

8. An unused movie ticket can sometimes be _____.

[03] Conversation

Getting Ready to Listen

A. Learn the words.

Key Vocabulary

application	a formal and usually written request for something such as a job
program	a series of classes or lectures
deadline	the time limit by which something must be done or completed by
statement	an expression of something such as a fact or intention

TOEFL Vocabulary

graduate	someone who has obtained a diploma or degree from a university or college
draft	a preliminary version of a piece of writing such as a speech, essay, or report
candidate	an applicant or suitable person for a job or program
submit	to hand something in for consideration, approval, or judgment
proceed	to continue with a course of action

B. Learn the question type.

TOEFL Question Type

Function

What can be inferred from the man/woman's response?

What is the purpose of the man/woman's response?

Why does the man/woman say this: ◯ ?

You will hear part of the conversation again.

- The question may focus on an idiom or expression that the speaker uses, so focus on understanding the informal language used.
- In conversations, speakers often ask questions to emphasize an emotion or to check another speaker's understanding.

Practice

A. **Listen to the first part of the conversation and choose the correct answers.**

Track 1-17

1. What is the main topic of this conversation?

   (A) Looking for advice on how to improve an application form.
   (B) Submitting an application form before a deadline.

2. How does the student explain what he would like?

   (A) He asks the professor to look at what he has done so far.
   (B) He tells the professor what he has done so far and asks for help.

Note-taking

B. **Listen to the full conversation and take notes.** Track 1-18

Man - Student	Woman - Professor
• Would like to speak about his application for _____ _____ • Has first _____ • Would like the professor to _____ _____ _____ _____ _____ _____	• The deadline for applications is _____ _____ _____ _____ _____ _____ _____ _____ _____ • Looks like a good _____

C. Choose the correct answers.

1. Why does the professor say this: ◯? **Track 1-19**

   (A) To make sure that the student knows that he does not have a lot of time left
   (B) To indicate that the student should submit the application now without changing it

2. What does the student imply when he says this: ◯? **Track 1-20**

   (A) That he does not care whether he is accepted by the program or not
   (B) That he would really like to be accepted for the graduate program

3. According to the professor, a good way to begin an application is with

   (A) an opening statement and then your main skills
   (B) your main skills and then your personal interests

TOEFL Vocabulary Practice

D. Fill in the blanks with the correct words.

graduate	candidates	draft	submit	proceed

1. People often write a first _____ of essays before they finish them.

2. A _____ can normally get a job when they finish college.

3. You must _____ an application if you would like a driver's license.

4. You have to get a ticket before you can _____ into a cinema.

5. There are often several _____ in an election.

Test

Listen to the conversation and take notes. **Track 1-21**

Woman - Student	Man - Professor
• Heard that the professor was looking for _____ _____	• Needs help with the research on _____ _____
• Was wondering if _____ _____ _____ _____ _____ _____ _____ _____ _____ _____ _____	• It is unpaid but _____ _____ _____ _____ _____ _____ • The deadline for the paper is at the end of _____ _____ _____

Choose the correct answers. **Track 1-22**

1. What is the conversation mainly about?

    (A) Getting better grades in class

    (B) An opportunity to help the professor with some research

    (C) The deadline for the professor's paper

    (D) What kind of paper the professor is writing

2. What does the student imply when she says this: ⌒ ?

    (A) That she would be a good person for the research position

    (B) That the professor doesn't know how to research

    (C) That the professor is helpless

    (D) That she is a professor

3. According to the professor, what are the advantages of the position?

    (A) Extra pay   (B) Extra credit and good grades

    (C) Experience and pay   (D) Better grades and experience

4. What can be inferred about the research position from the conversation? Place a checkmark in the correct box.

	True	False
The student will be paid to carry out the research		
It will be good experience for the student		
The deadline for the paper is in the middle of next year		
Many students have applied for the position		

Lecture - Botany

Getting Ready to Listen

A. Learn the words.

Key Vocabulary

human	man; mankind; people
crops	plants, usually fruit or vegetables, grown together for use by people
maize	corn; a yellow cereal
poison	a substance that is harmful or can kill

TOEFL Vocabulary

disease	an illness; a thing that makes living things unwell
biological	to do with life, with the study of living things
ecosystem	a group of living things living/working together in nature
organism	a living thing
produce	fruit or vegetables that are sold fresh

B. Learn the question type.

TOEFL Question Type

Function

What can be inferred from the professor/student's response?

What is the purpose of the professor/student's response?

Why does the professor say this: ◯ ?

You will hear part of the lecture again.

- In lectures, speakers often ask rhetorical questions to emphasize a point or check the students' understanding.
- In lectures, speakers often tell stories to give examples or to describe a process.
- Refer to your notes to see how the speaker's words best relate to the main idea of the lecture.

Practice

A. **Listen to the first part of the lecture and choose the correct answers.** `Track 1-23`

1. What is the main topic of this lecture?

   (A) Human illnesses   (B) Plant diseases

2. What are the key points in this lecture?

   (A) Plant diseases are a biological problem, which are spread by germs and are hard to get rid of; the best solution is to prevent the diseases.

   (B) Germs affect different plant parts and they are an important part of the ecosystem; the best solution is to kill the diseased plants.

3. How does the professor describe the main topic?

   (A) By defining concepts   (B) By talking about problems and solutions

4. Choose the best note-taking diagram for this lecture.

   (A) Venn Diagram   (B) Ordering Diagram   (C) Problem and Solution Diagram

Note-taking

B. **Draw the diagram chosen in question 4. Then insert the information from questions 1 and 2.**

C. **Now listen to the full lecture and complete your notes.** `Track 1-24`

D. Choose the correct answers.

1. Listen again to part of the lecture. Then answer the question. ◯ `Track 1-25`

What does the professor mean when he says this: ◯ ?

(A) He means that plant diseases are a very expensive problem.

(B) He wants to emphasize that plant diseases are a very serious problem.

2. According to the professor, which of the following is true about farming crops?

(A) Diseases can spread easily if farmers grow one crop.

(B) Diseases can't spread easily if farmers grow one crop.

3. Why does the professor say this: ◯ ? `Track 1-26`

(A) He wants to make sure no one ever uses poison.

(B) He wants to make students aware of the dangers of using poison.

TOEFL Vocabulary Practice

E. Fill in the blanks with the correct words.

organisms	disease	produce	biological	ecosystem

1. A farmers' market usually sells fresh _____.

2. Sharks seem dangerous but they are a big part of the ocean's _____.

3. Cancer is a terrible _____ that kills many people.

4. Scientists are studying the _____ causes of cancer.

5. Plankton are tiny _____ that live in the sea and are eaten by whales.

Test

Listen to the lecture and take notes. **Track 1-27**

Insects

- Eat plants
- Make their nests and lay eggs inside plants
- Carry disease
- Cause a lot of damage.

Problem	Solution
Insects damage plants • They eat plants ——→	Check plants daily

Choose the correct answers. **Track 1-28**

1. What is the lecture mainly about?

(A) How insects spread plant diseases
(B) The damages caused to crops by locusts
(C) Problems insects cause and how to stop them
(D) The environmental dangers of plant poisons

2. What is the professor's attitude toward insects?

(A) He thinks they are interesting.
(B) He is scared of them.
(C) He thinks they are harmful.
(D) He finds them very special.

3. Why does the professor tell students that just like plant diseases, insects are also a biological problem and part of the ecosystem?

   (A) Because he thinks it is an interesting co-incidence
   (B) Because he wants to explain that the only threats to plants are natural ones
   (C) Because he wants to emphasize that diseases are not the only natural problem facing plants
   (D) Because he wants students to see that everything they study has to do with ecosystems

4. According to the professor, if you get a new plant you should first

   (A) keep it to one side for about a month
   (B) spray it with poison immediately
   (C) pull off all its dead leaves
   (D) keep watering it for a month

5. Why does the professor say this: 🎧 ?

   (A) To encourage students to use poison if need be
   (B) Because he is very scared of people who use poison
   (C) Because poison always ends up killing your plants
   (D) To stress that poison should only be used if nothing else works

6. According to the professor, what are the likely outcomes of using poison on plants? Choose 2 answers.

   (A) Plants could be harmed or die.
   (B) Insects will get used to the poison.
   (C) The environment will be harmed.
   (D) The soil and air will be full of dead insects.

Check-up

A. Choose the correct answers.

1. When answering a conversation function question
   (A) choose an answer that best explains why a speaker uses a certain idiom or expression
   (B) refer to your notes for the central problem the student wants to solve
   (C) choose the answer that best explains the speaker's opinion
   (D) refer to your notes for key words under headings that support the main idea

2. What should you do when answering a lecture function question?
   (A) Refer to your notes for the professor's reaction to advice.
   (B) Pick the answer that details the pattern to which the points of the lecture are presented.
   (C) Refer to your notes for important details; the test will not ask for minor details.
   (D) Pick an answer that best explains why the professor tells a certain story.

Key Vocabulary Practice

B. Fill in the blanks with the correct words.

application	maize	program	deadline
statement	human	crops	poison

1. When you decide to be a student you must choose a(n) _____ to study.

2. The Egyptians were some of the first people to cultivate _____.

3. _____ is the staple food in many South American countries.

4. If you want to apply for a job, you must complete a job _____ form.

5. If you give evidence to the police you must give a(n) _____ about what you know.

6. Hitler used a(n) _____ called cyanide to kill himself.

7. Journalists must finish writing newspaper stories by a(n) _____ in order for them to be printed on time.

8. Many scientists believe _____ beings developed from monkeys.

[04] Conversation

Getting Ready to Listen

A. Learn the words.

Key Vocabulary

canteen	a cafeteria, especially in a school or workplace
complaint	a statement expressing discontent or unhappiness about a situation
serve	to present food or drink
allergy	an unusual sensitivity or physical reaction to a normally harmless substance

TOEFL Vocabulary

elaborate	to give more detail about something
occasion	a particular time when something happens
commitment	a responsibility to a specific appointment, person, or thing
pressure	to make somebody do something
inspiration	stimulation to come up with ideas

B. Learn the question type.

TOEFL Question Type

Attitude

What is the man/woman's opinion of X?

What can be inferred about the student?

- Take note of any strong emotions or opinions mentioned by the speakers.
- Pay attention to the tone of the speakers' voices as they respond to each other.

Practice

A. **Listen to the first part of the conversation and choose the correct answers.**
Track 1-29

1. What is the main topic of this conversation?

    (A) Making a complaint about the head of the canteen

    (B) Making a complaint about the canteen menu

2. How does the student explain his problem?

    (A) He describes the food that he cannot eat.

    (B) He lists all of the food that he can eat.

Note-taking

B. **Listen to the full conversation and take notes.** Track 1-30

Man - Student	Woman - Head of Canteen
• Would like to complain about _____	• Would like the student to _____
	• The canteen does have _____
	• Has a commitment to _____

C. Choose the correct answers.

1. What was the head of the canteen's attitude toward the menu complaint made by the student?

(A) She was insistent that the canteen does cater for students with allergies every day.

(B) She was frustrated because it is very difficult to cater for people with allergies and to keep everyone else happy with the menu, too.

2. What was the student's opinion of the wheat-free food served by the canteen?

(A) He was happy that there was a good selection, but more choice would be better.

(B) He was frustrated that the choice of food was very limited every day.

3. What does the student mean when he says this: ? **Track 1-31**

(A) That it should be easy for the canteen staff to find good wheat-free recipes

(B) That he thinks that it shouldn't be difficult to make food that many people can enjoy

TOEFL Vocabulary Practice

D. Fill in the blanks with the correct words.

elaborate	occasion	commitment	pressure	inspiration

1. Many artists get their _____ from nature.

2. Parents often have to _____ their children to clean their rooms.

3. To get somebody to understand what you are saying, sometimes you have to _____ more.

4. It is a very special _____ when two people get married.

5. Getting a pet dog can be a big _____ for a family.

Test

Listen to the conversation and take notes. Track 1-32

Woman - Student	Man - Canteen Employee
• Is a _____ • Is wondering what _____ _____ • Will not eat _____ _____ _____ _____ _____ _____	• Thinks a vegan is like _____ _____ • On today's menu, there are _____ _____ _____ _____ _____ _____ _____

Choose the correct answers. Track 1-33

1. According to the student, what does a vegan avoid eating?

(A) Animal meat
(B) Any kind of food that comes from an animal
(C) Any food made near animals
(D) Vegetables and rice

2. Why is the student talking to the canteen worker?

(A) To tell him that she is a vegan
(B) To complain about the food on the menu that day
(C) To find out what food on the menu is suitable for vegans
(D) To ask him to improve the menu

3. What is the canteen worker's opinion of the student being a vegan?

(A) He thinks it is a silly thing to do.
(B) He has respect for how hard it must be.
(C) He thinks that the canteen can't accommodate her.
(D) He wants to become a vegan as well.

4. How does the student raise the issue that the canteen does not serve a lot of food for vegans?

(A) She explains what a vegan is to the canteen worker.
(B) She emphasizes that she understands how the canteen has to keep everybody happy.
(C) She misleads the canteen worker to believe that she is allergic to all food that comes from animals.
(D) She asks what food is suitable for vegans on the menu that day.

Lecture - Chemistry

Getting Ready to Listen

A. Learn the words.

Key Vocabulary	
pure	not mixed with other substances
type	a number of things that are part of a group, or category
atom	a tiny particle that makes up matter
join	to come together; to become part of something

TOEFL Vocabulary	
element	a basic substance that cannot be separated
compound	a substance consisting of different elements that have chemically joined
mixture	a substance formed when two other substances mix together but do not join atoms
periodic table	a chart that lists the elements according to atomic number
despite	in contradiction to

B. Learn the question type.

TOEFL Question Type

Attitude

What can be inferred from the professor/student's response?

What does the professor mean when he/she says this: 🎧 ?

- Some questions will replay part of the lecture again.
- Pay attention to the words and phrases spoken just before and after a repeated comment to understand its context.

Practice

A. **Listen to the first part of the lecture and choose the correct answers.** `Track 1-34`

1. What is the main topic of this lecture?

   (A) Atoms   (B) Substances

2. What are the key points in this lecture?

   (A) What pure, impure, and mixed substances are
   (B) What elements, compounds, and mixtures are

3. How does the professor describe the main topic?

   (A) By presenting problems and their solutions
   (B) By discussing each category in turn

4. Choose the best note-taking diagram for this lecture.

   (A) Categorizing   (B) Ordering Diagram   (C) Problem and Solution
       Diagram   Diagram

Note-taking

B. **Draw the diagram chosen in question 4. Then insert the information from questions 1 and 2.**

C. **Now listen to the full lecture and complete your notes.** `Track 1-35`

D. Choose the correct answers.

1. What is the professor's opinion of the distinction between elements, compounds, and mixtures?

   (A) It is complicated.   (B) It is important.

2. What is the professor's opinion of separating salt from water?

   (A) It is easy.   (B) It is difficult.

3. Why does the professor say this: ⌒ ?   **Track 1-36**

   (A) To illicit a response from students

   (B) To indicate that the upcoming information will be important

TOEFL Vocabulary Practice

E. Fill in the blanks with the correct words.

element	compound	mixture	periodic table	despite

1. Sugar is a(n) _____. It is made up of carbon, hydrogen, and oxygen. They are not easily separated.

2. According to the _____, the atomic number of iron is 26.

3. _____ poor attendance due to illness, it is possible to get a good mark in a class.

4. Gold is a(n) _____. It is pure and cannot be broken down.

5. Sea water is a(n) _____ of salt and water. They can be separated easily.

Test

Listen to the lecture and take notes. **Track 1-37**

The Periodic Table

- Periods—rows

- Groups—columns

- Series—colors

The Periodic Table
Over 100 elements
Created by Mendeleev in 1869

- 2 elements that don't fit

Choose the correct answers. **Track 1-38**

1. What is the lecture mainly about?

(A) The layout of the periodic table

(B) How Mendeleev improved the periodic table

(C) Current problems with the periodic table

(D) Predictions for the future of the periodic table

2. What do the different colors of the periodic table represent?

(A) Categories of elements   (B) Groups of elements

(C) Periods of elements   (D) Behaviors of elements

3. What is the professor's attitude toward Mendeleev?

(A) He thinks he has not been given proper credit.

(B) He thinks that he does not deserve credit for inventing the periodic table.

(C) He thinks that he stole someone else's idea for the ordering of the elements.

(D) He thinks he made an important contribution to science.

4. How does the professor organize the information on the periodic table?

(A) By discussing each period and group one by one

(B) By first outlining the format, then discussing its development

(C) By demonstrating what can be learned about each element from its block

(D) By outlining the history of the development of the table

5. Why does the professor say this: 🎧 ?

(A) To suggest that some elements are kept secret

(B) To imply that there may be more that haven't been discovered

(C) To invite students to think of new elements to add

(D) To demonstrate the controversial nature of the topic

6. Choose whether each of the following can be determined from an element's row, column, or color.

	Row	Column	Color
Group			
Period			
Category			
Behavior when mixed with water			

Check-up

A. **Choose the correct answers.**

1. When answering a conversation attitude question
   (A) choose the answer that explains the main problem the students want solved
   (B) refer to your notes for any strong emotions or opinions mentioned by the speakers
   (C) choose the answer that puts the steps of a sequence in the correct order
   (D) refer to your notes for key words under headings that support the main idea

2. What should you do when answering a lecture attitude question?
   (A) Listen carefully for the main purpose of the lecture.
   (B) Listen carefully to the words and phrases spoken just before and after a repeated comment.
   (C) Listen carefully for minor details about the main topic of the lecture.
   (D) Listen carefully for the correct sequence of steps in a process described by the professor.

Key Vocabulary Practice

B. **Fill in the blanks with the correct words.**

pure	canteen	type	served
atoms	complaint	allergy	join

1. All matter is made up of _____.

2. If you are treated badly by staff in a shop or restaurant, it is normal to make a _____ to the manager.

3. The substance is _____. There is nothing added to it.

4. When two or more elements _____ together, they become a compound.

5. Some people have a(n) _____ to wasps and bees so bad that they can die if stung by one.

6. In popular, expensive restaurants, the food _____ should taste very nice.

7. People who like the same _____ of music tend to get along well.

8. Most schools and large workplaces have a(n) _____ where you can get your lunch.

[05] Conversation

Getting Ready to Listen

A. Learn the words.

Key Vocabulary

ticket	a paper notice indicating a parking offense or traffic violation has been committed and a fine is due
permit	a document that states you have been granted permission
warning	a notice or caution of a violation that has been or may be committed
handicap	an injury, illness, or defect that hinders someone or something

TOEFL Vocabulary

violation	the breaking of the law or rules set in place
security	someone who protects and keeps the law
subsequent	happening after something
urge	to encourage strongly
license	a printed document that gives official permission to do something

B. Learn the question type.

TOEFL Question Type

Organization

How is the discussion organized?

Why does the man/woman discuss X?

Why does the man/woman mention X?

• Organization questions are more commonly asked after lectures rather than conversations.

• Refer to your notes for any connections between parts of the conversation.

Practice

A. Listen to the first part of the conversation and choose the correct answers.

Track 1-39

1. What is the main topic of this lecture?
    (A) A student not wanting to pay her speeding violation
    (B) A student wanting to take care of a parking violation

2. How does the employee explain why she received a parking ticket?
    (A) By asking the student how she received the ticket and then explaining to her what the problem was with her answer
    (B) By telling the student she was not paying attention to the appropriate signs

Note-taking

B. Listen to the full conversation and take notes. Track 1-40

Woman - Student	Man - University Employee
• Needs to pay _____ _____	• Need a permit to _____ _____
• Has hurt her leg and _____ _____	• It isn't a ticket; it is _____ _____ _____ _____ _____
• Received ticket for _____ _____ _____ _____ _____ _____ _____	• With note from doctor, can get handicapped permit _____ _____ _____

C. Choose the correct answers.

1. How is the conversation organized?

(A) In the order the events took place

(B) By the employee asking a question leading to the details of the event

2. What is the student's attitude toward the male employee?

(A) Frustrated that she received a ticket

(B) Very willing to pay for the mistake she made

3. Why does the employee discuss permits?

(A) To explain how useful they are

(B) To encourage the student to buy one

TOEFL Vocabulary Practice

D. Fill in the blanks with the correct words.

license	subsequent	urge	violation	security

1. All banks have night _____ on duty.

2. Teachers _____ students to study hard for important exams.

3. At the age of 16, you can apply for your driver's _____.

4. _____ tickets could lead to further punishment.

5. Speeding on the university campus is a(n) _____.

Test

Listen to the conversation and take notes. Track 1-41

Man - Student	Woman - University Employee
• Needs to purchase _____ _____	• Needs driver's _____ _____
• Got a warning from _____ _____ _____ _____ _____ _____ _____ _____	_____ _____ _____ _____ _____ _____ _____ _____

Choose the correct answers. Track 1-42

1. What is the conversation mainly about?

(A) The privileges of having parking permit

(B) Purchasing a parking permit

(C) Parking violations

(D) Where the student needs to go to purchase a permit

2. Why does the employee discuss the appropriate location to hang the parking permit?

(A) To fill some time while the permit was being made

(B) Just in case the student didn't know

(C) To make sure the student hangs it in a visible spot to avoid receiving a ticket

(D) She was instructed to

3. Listen again to part of the lecture. Then answer the question.

Why does the student say this: ?

(A) To make sure the employee knows he has a valid reason for receiving a handicap permit

(B) The employee asked for the doctor's note at the beginning of the conversation

(C) To let the employee know he goes to the doctor often

(D) To look for some empathy from the employee

4. According to the employee, which of the following is true?

(A) With a handicap permit, you can park anywhere.

(B) You can place the permit on rear-view mirror or in the back window.

(C) After receiving a warning, the student's next violation will result in a ticket.

(D) You have to have a written note from your doctor and a university employee to receive the permit.

60 | Listening |

Lecture - Business

Getting Ready to Listen

A. Learn the words.

Key Vocabulary

patent	a document that protects ideas from being copied
retail	the sale of products, like clothes or shoes, in small quantities directly to the customer
rival	someone who competes with others
board	a small group of people who control and run an organization

TOEFL Vocabulary

document	a paper that records information about something
procedure	the steps taken to do something
complex	involved; not simple
seek	to look for something; to ask for something
approve	to agree to; to allow something

B. Learn the question type.

TOEFL Question Type

Organization

How does the professor organize the information about X that he/she presents to the class?

How is the discussion organized?

Why does the professor mention X?

- Organization questions are more commonly asked after lectures rather than conversations.
- Look at your notes for any pattern to how the points of the lecture were presented (e.g., from most to least important, according to time, etc.)

Practice

A. **Listen to the first part of the lecture and choose the correct answers.** `Track 1-43`

1. What is the main topic of the lecture?

   (A) Patents   (B) Business rivals

2. What are the key points in this lecture?

   (A) Sheri, who made "Jibbitz" shoes, made a lot of money but had many rivals.
   (B) It's important to get a patent document written to protect a good business
   idea.

3. How does the professor describe the main topic?

   (A) By comparing and contrasting   (B) As a step-by-step process

4. Choose the best note-taking diagram for this lecture.

   (A) Problem and Solution   (B) Categorizing   (C) Ordering Diagram
   Diagram   Diagram

Note-taking

B. **Draw the diagram chosen in question 4. Then insert the information from
questions 1 and 2.**

C. **Now listen to the full lecture and complete your notes.** `Track 1-44`

D. Choose the correct answers.

1. Why did the professor discuss Sheri's "Jibbitz" shoes?

   (A) She was worried about someone stealing Sheri's idea.

   (B) She wanted to give an example of someone who needed to patent their idea.

2. Listen again to part of the lecture. Then answer the question. 🎧 **Track 1-45**
   What is the professor's attitude toward business rivals who steal ideas?

   (A) She thinks they are dishonest.   (B) She admires them.

3. Why does the professor end her lecture by telling students a patent lasts 20 years?

   (A) To explain why it is so complex to get a patent

   (B) Because she thinks it is too long a time to have a patent

TOEFL Vocabulary Practice

E. Fill in the blanks with the correct words.

approve	document	complex	seek	procedure

1. The USA's Declaration of Independence is an important historical _____.

2. A heart transplant is a difficult medical _____.

3. The causes of the First World War are very _____.

4. The Spanish commander Cortez went to _____ gold in America.

5. In many cultures, your parents must _____ of your partner before you can marry them.

Test

🎧 Listen to the lecture and take notes. `Track 1-46`

Starting a Business

1. Get a patent

2. Get money

3. Get a place

4. Get workers

Starting a Business

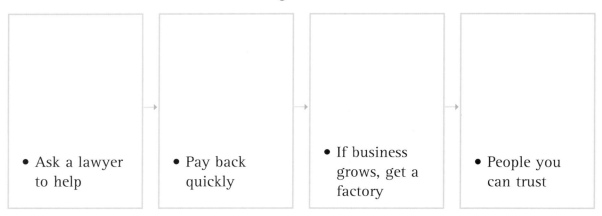

- Ask a lawyer to help → - Pay back quickly → - If business grows, get a factory → - People you can trust

Choose the correct answers. `Track 1-47`

1. What is the lecture mainly about?

(A) Starting a business

(B) Getting a patent

(C) Buying a factory

(D) Borrowing money

2. Why does the professor start the lecture talking about getting patents?

(A) Because she wants to make sure students understood her last lecture
(B) Because she believes it is the first and most important step when starting a business
(C) Because she finds patents the most interesting thing in business studies
(D) Because the patent process is so hard to understand

3. According to the professor, one of the reasons you need money to start a business is

(A) to buy a patent
(B) to pay off rivals
(C) to buy big factories
(D) to pay your staff

4. Listen again to part of the lecture. Then answer the question. ◯

What does the professor imply when she says this: ◯ ?

(A) That banks run the world and have all the business power
(B) That we should be very careful when we borrow money
(C) That banks cheat people out of money by charging high interest
(D) That there is no kindness in the world and that we pay for everything

5. Listen again to part of the lecture. Then answer the question. ◯

What is the professor's attitude toward workers?

(A) She thinks that good workers are rare.
(B) She believes all workers are lazy.
(C) She thinks a good worker will be expensive to hire.
(D) She believes workers want to steal from you.

6. According to the professor, what is the likely outcome of getting a patent, some money, a good work space, and good workers?

(A) You will owe a bank a lot of money.
(B) You will stop all your rivals.
(C) You will run a successful business.
(D) You will own a big factory.

Check-up

A. Choose the correct answers.

1. When answering a conversation organization question
   (A) pay attention to the words and phrases spoken just before and after a repeated comment
   (B) look in your notes for any rhetorical questions asked by the speakers
   (C) refer to your notes for any pattern to how the points are presented, such as chronologically or by importance
   (D) listen carefully for minor details about the main topic of the lecture

2. What should you do when answering a lecture organization question?
   (A) Refer to your notes for any strong emotions expressed by the speakers.
   (B) Look at your notes for any pattern to how the points of the lecture are presented.
   (C) Refer to your notes for any rhetorical questions asked by the professor.
   (D) Look in your notes for repeated content words or phrases to give you a clue about the main idea.

Key Vocabulary Practice

B. Fill in the blanks with the correct words.

retail	permits	patents	handicap
rivals	board	warning	ticket

1. Students need _____ to park on campus.

2. Bill Gates was wise to get _____ for many Microsoft products.

3. Young students often receive a _____ before they are punished.

4. All big companies have a _____ of directors to run them.

5. The _____ industry in the USA competes with imported Chinese products.

6. Police may give a _____ for speeding in a school zone.

7. Japan and South Korea are big _____ in soccer.

8. A student's _____ allows him or her to have special access to the elevators.

[06] Conversation

Getting Ready to Listen

A. Learn the words.

Key Vocabulary

computer crash	when a computer is overloaded and stops working
rewrite	to redo an already written paper or document
backup	to make a copy or copies of computer data in case the original data is lost or damaged
disk	a device that is used to store information from a computer

TOEFL Vocabulary

time consuming	to fill time with a large amount of something; to take a lot of time
unacceptable	not satisfactory
nonetheless	however; on the other hand
mark	to grade
credit	equivalent to a grade; recognition for something being completed

B. Learn the question type.

TOEFL Question Type

Content

What is the likely outcome of doing X then Y?

What does the man/woman imply about X?

Indicate whether each of the following was mentioned in the conversation.

- Questions asking for information to be organized into a table are more common after lectures.
- Look at your notes for relationships between the points made in the conversation.
- Pay attention to advice given and reaction to the advice for help on prediction questions.

Practice

Track 2-1

A. Listen to the first part of the conversation and choose the correct answers.

1. What is the main topic of this conversation?

   (A) The student wanting to redo her project

   (B) The student wanting to receive an extension on her project

2. How does the student explain the problem?

   (A) By giving specific reasons why she didn't hand the project in

   (B) By explaining the reasons why her computer crashed

Note-taking

B. Listen to the full conversation and take notes. Track 2-2

Woman - Student	Man - Professor
• Project due today but _____ _____	• Understands, but _____ _____
• Computer _____ _____ _____	• Can't give _____ _____
• Could rewrite and _____ _____ _____ _____	_____ _____ _____ _____

C. Choose the correct answers.

1. What is the timely outcome of starting earlier on a paper and backing it up on a disk?

   (A) This problem would be avoided.
   (B) This problem would still occur.

2. Why does the professor discuss the importance of backing up work?

   (A) If the student had made a backup disk, she wouldn't need an extension.
   (B) If a backup disk is made, then the student could use the project in future classes.

3. Which of the following was mentioned in the conversation?

   (A) The professor will allow the student to turn in the project a week late.
   (B) The professor will only give half credit for the project.

TOEFL Vocabulary Practice

D. Fill in the blanks with the correct words.

time consuming	unacceptable	nonetheless	marking	credit

1. Sometimes, a professor will give extra _____ to any student that turns a project in early.

2. Showing up to class late is not allowed. _____, going to class late cannot be avoided under certain circumstances.

3. Arriving late to work is _____.

4. Teachers are often very busy _____ papers around report card time.

5. The majority of college students would say that studying is very _____.

Test

Listen to the conversation and take notes.   **Track 2-3**

Woman - Professor	Man - Student
• Noticed essay was _____ • Irresponsibility is _____ _____ _____ _____ _____ _____	• Needs an _____ _____ _____ _____ _____ _____ _____

Choose the correct answers.   **Track 2-4**

1. Why does the student need to speak to the professor?

  (A) He picked an inappropriate topic for his final project and needs help picking a new one.

  (B) He missed the class and needs the lecture notes.

  (C) He forgot his essay was due and needs an extension.

  (D) He is failing the class and needs to be advised on what to do.

2. What can be inferred about the student?

  (A) The student is under a lot of stress.

  (B) The student is not managing his time well.

  (C) The student does not care about this class.

  (D) Both A and B

3. According to the professor, what is unacceptable?

  (A) The student coming to his office not during office hours

  (B) The student forgetting about the due date of the project

  (C) The student wanting special privileges

  (D) The student coming to class without talking to the professor first

4. What is the professor's attitude toward the student?
  (A) Upset   (B) Relaxed
  (C) Lenient   (D) Excited

Lecture - Geology

Getting Ready to Listen

A. Learn the words.

Key Vocabulary

igneous	rock formed from cooled liquid rock
sedimentary	rock formed from layers of rock pieces
metamorphic	rock changed because of heat
magma	hot liquid rock

TOEFL Vocabulary

constantly	continuously; without interruption
cycle	a recurring sequence of events
illustrate	to demonstrate or show
drift	to move aimlessly
crystal	a shiny rock with a certain arrangement of atoms

B. Learn the question type.

TOEFL Question Type

Content

In the lecture, the professor describes X. Indicate whether each of the following is mentioned. Based on information in the lecture, indicate whether each sentence below describes X, Y, or Z. Match each X with the correct classification.

- Questions asking for information to be organized into a table are more common after lectures.
- It is important to take well-organized notes while listening in order to be able to refer to them when answering organization questions.
- Be sure to order steps in a process or organize details into categories as you listen.

Practice

A. Listen to the first part of the lecture and choose the correct answers. Track 2-5

1. What is the main topic of this lecture?

    (A) The rock cycle   (B) Continental drift

2. What are the key points in this lecture?

    (A) How the Earth's crust is formed

    (B) How igneous, sedimentary, and metamorphic rocks are formed

3. How does the professor describe the main topic?

    (A) By showing what causes each type of rock to form

    (B) By comparing and contrasting the different types of rock

4. Choose the best note-taking diagram for this lecture.

    (A) Venn Diagram   (B) Problem and Solution   (C) Cause and Effect
                                                  Diagram   Diagram

---

Note-taking

B. Draw the diagram chosen in question 4. Then insert the information from questions 1 and 2.

C. Now listen to the full lecture and complete your notes. Track 2-6

D. Choose the correct answers.

1. What is the likely outcome of heating rock?

    (A) Sedimentary rock will be created.

    (B) Metamorphic rock will be created.

2. What is the likely outcome of cooling magma?

    (A) Igneous rock will be created.

    (B) Metamorphic rock will be created.

3. Why does the professor mention the division of the Earth's crust into plates?

    (A) To demonstrate the force that drives the rock cycle

    (B) To explain what causes rock to heat up to create metamorphic rock

TOEFL Vocabulary Practice

E. Fill in the blanks with the correct words.

constantly	cycle	illustrate	drift	crystal

1. Economists use graphs to _____ trends in the economy.

2. Water changes form as it moves through the water _____.

3. A branch will _____ away if thrown in a river.

4. Because of its unique look, _____ is an expensive type of rock.

5. A mill turns _____ because of a river. It never stops.

Test

🎧 Listen to the lecture and take notes. **Track 2-7**

Continental Drift

- Plates crash together = mountains

- Plates moving apart = volcanoes

- Plates sliding past each other = earthquakes

Continental Drift

Cause		Effect
Plates crashing together	→	
	→	
	→	

Choose the correct answers. **Track 2-8**

1. What is the lecture mainly about?

    (A) The danger of volcanoes

    (B) The danger of earthquakes

    (C) Why the continents drift apart

    (D) The effects of continental drift

2. What is the likely outcome of two plates sliding past each other?

(A) Earthquakes   (B) Volcanoes

(C) Mountains   (D) Rifts

3. What is the professor's attitude toward continental drift?

(A) She thinks it is dangerous.

(B) She thinks it is not true.

(C) She thinks it is a complicated subject.

(D) She thinks it tells us a lot about the Earth.

4. How does the professor organize the information about continental drift?

(A) By talking about the scientist who came up with the theory

(B) By demonstrating the different effects of continental drift

(C) By showing how the Earth's continents seem to fit together like a puzzle

(D) By showing a map of what the world looked like before the continents split into different plates

5. Why does the professor say this: ⌒ ?

(A) To give an example of the disastrous consequences of continental drift

(B) To illustrate the phenomenon of which she is speaking

(C) To show how two local plates happen to be moving

(D) To disprove the theory of continental drift with a hypothetical example

6. In the lecture, the professor discusses the different effects of continental drift. Indicate whether each of the following was mentioned.

	Yes	No
Formation of mountains		
Formation of rifts		
Tornadoes		
Earthquakes		

Check-up

A. Choose the correct answers.

1. When answering a conversation content question
   - (A) look in your notes for any rhetorical questions asked by the speakers
   - (B) look in your notes for relationships between the points made in the conversation
   - (C) look in your notes for the central problem the student wants to solve
   - (D) look in your notes for repeated content words or phrases to give you a clue about the main idea

2. What should you do when answering a lecture content question?
   - (A) Take note of as many minor details as possible so you won't miss anything when answering the question.
   - (B) Look in your notes to figure out why the professor tells a certain story during the lecture.
   - (C) Take well-organized notes while listening so you can refer to them when answering the question.
   - (D) Look in your notes to figure out what the professor is mainly discussing in the lecture.

Key Vocabulary Practice

B. Fill in the blanks with the correct words.

computer crash	igneous	rewrite	backup
sedimentary	metamorphic	magma	disk

1. Students often _____ their work just in case they lose it.

2. A computer _____ is a school supply sold at the bookstore.

3. _____ rock is formed when tiny pieces of rock stick together.

4. If a student doesn't do well on an essay, a professor will sometimes make them _____ it.

5. _____ is liquid rock found beneath the surface of the Earth.

6. _____ rock is formed when magma cools.

7. _____ rock is formed when rock is heated up.

8. It is common for a(n) _____ to happen when you put too much information on a computer.

[Review 1]

Listen to the conversation and take notes.　Track 2-9

Woman - Student	Man - Professor
• She is applying to _____ • She thinks she did well _____ _____ _____ _____ _____ _____	• He thinks she is a good _____ _____ _____ _____ _____ _____ _____

Choose the correct answers.　Track 2-10

1. What are the speakers mainly discussing?

(A) The girl's application for grad school

(B) The pressure students are under in their senior year

(C) The procedure for applying for financial aid

(D) The likelihood of the girl being accepted to grad school

2. What does the woman still need to do?

(A) Take the GRE　　　　　　　　(B) Ask for a letter of recommendation

(C) Have her transcripts sent　　　(D) Complete her application

3. What is the professor's opinion of the woman?

(A) He thinks she is a good student.

(B) He thinks she won't get into grad school.

(C) He thinks she is stressed out.

(D) He thinks she needs to improve her marks.

4. Why does the professor say this: ⌒?

(A) To suggest that the woman should speak to a counselor

(B) To show empathy and offer assistance

(C) To express his opinion that standards are too high

(D) To demonstrate the dangers of working too hard

Listen to the lecture and take notes. Track 2-11

Green Architecture

• Energy

• Orientation

• Materials

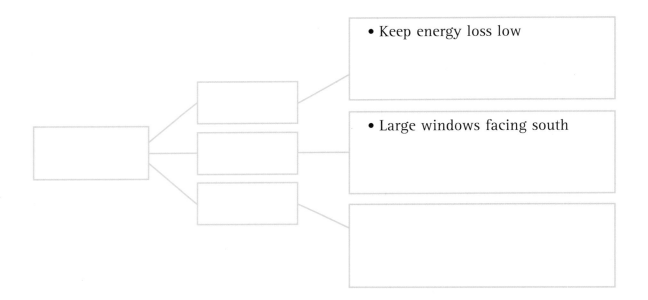

• Keep energy loss low

• Large windows facing south

Choose the correct answers. Track 2-12

1. What is the lecture mainly about?

(A) The popularity of Green Architecture
(B) The importance of Green Architecture
(C) Problems with Green Architecture
(D) Key considerations in Green Architecture

2. What is the professor's attitude toward Green Architecture?

(A) He thinks it's a worthy pursuit.
(B) He thinks it's a waste of money.
(C) He thinks more research should be done.
(D) He thinks it's ineffective.

3. What is the likely outcome of poorly insulating your home?

(A) It will lose energy.   (B) It will save money.
(C) It will pollute the air.   (D) It will waste resources.

4. Where should you install large windows in order to get heat from the Sun?

(A) On the north side   (B) On the south side
(C) On the east side   (D) On the west side

5. Listen again to part of the lecture. Then answer the question.

Why does the professor say this: ?

(A) To suggest that they are radical
(B) To inspire students to do the same
(C) To explain their motivation
(D) To make a moral judgment

6. How is the lecture organized?

(A) By contrasting Green Architecture with traditional architecture
(B) By outlining the history of Green Architecture
(C) By describing three main elements of Green Architecture in turn
(D) By showing how Green Architecture solves a specific problem

🎧 Listen to the lecture and take notes. `Track 2-13`

Sole Proprietorship
• Owner responsible for debts
• Owner pays taxes on income

Corporation
• Company responsible for debts
• Company pays taxes

Types of Ownership

Sole Proprietorship   Corporation

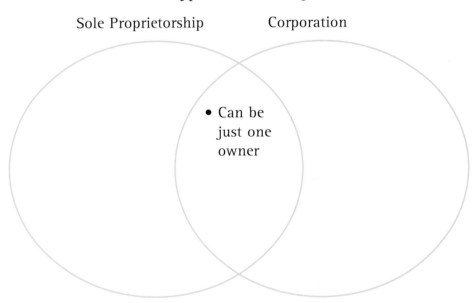

• Can be just one owner

Choose the correct answers. `Track 2-14`

1. What is the lecture mainly about?

(A) How to run a business
(B) How to get a business license
(C) Decision making in business
(D) Types of business ownership

2. How is the discussion organized?

    (A) By comparing and contrasting the types of ownership

    (B) By discussing problems and suggesting solutions

    (C) By outlining factors in the decision-making process

    (D) By explaining each category in turn

3. What do a sole proprietorship and a corporation have in common?

    (A) Both offer protection to the owner from debts incurred by the company

    (B) Both result in higher taxes because the business is taxed in addition to the owner

    (C) Both can be owned by just one person

    (D) Both can be owned by multiple parties

4. What will happen if a sole proprietor borrows money for her business and the business fails?

    (A) Nothing will happen.   (B) She will have to pay it back.

    (C) She will sell the business.   (D) She will lower prices.

5. What is the professor's opinion of corporations?

    (A) They don't pay enough taxes.

    (B) They are safer than sole proprietorships.

    (C) They are irresponsible in their business practices.

    (D) They are easier to run than sole proprietorships.

6. What does the professor imply when he says this: 🎧 ?

    (A) People are unlikely to go into business without backers.

    (B) There are other options if there is more than one owner.

    (C) These are the only reasonable options for partners.

    (D) It is dangerous to go into business with other people.

Lecture 3

Listen to the lecture and take notes. `Track 2-15`

Plants Need

- Energy
- Water
- Nutrients
- To reproduce

Problem	Solution
⟶	Get it from sunlight
⟶	
⟶	
⟶	

Choose the correct answers. `Track 2-16`

1. What is the lecture mainly about?

(A) How plants survive both as individuals and as species
(B) Specific problems faced by pollinating plants
(C) How plants survive when there is little water
(D) How water plants are different from land plants

2. How does the professor organize the information about plant survival?

    (A) By presenting problems and showing how plants adapt
    (B) By contrasting the plant kingdom with the animal kingdom
    (C) By outlining the life cycle of a particular flower
    (D) By demonstrating how plants cope with a lack of water

3. How do plants get nutrients?

    (A) Through their petals   (B) Through their roots
    (C) From the Sun   (D) From water

4. What is the likely outcome of denying a plant water?

    (A) It will die.   (B) It will stop growing.
    (C) It will need more sunlight.   (D) It will need more nutrients.

5. What is the professor's attitude toward plants?

    (A) She thinks they are too fragile to survive without human help.
    (B) She thinks they should be protected from harmful UV rays.
    (C) She thinks they evolve faster than animal species.
    (D) She thinks they are integral to the ecosystem.

6. Why does the professor say this: ☊ ?

    (A) To explain why plants evolved the way that they did
    (B) To show how plants are often forgotten in the ecosystem
    (C) To demonstrate why so many plants are endangered
    (D) To introduce the topic of plant survival

Conversation 2

Listen to the conversation and take notes. **Track 2-17**

Man - Student	Woman - Receptionist
• Seeking _____ • Explains that he is on _____ _____ _____ _____ _____ _____	• Tells him he's _____ _____ _____ _____ _____ _____ _____

Choose the correct answers. **Track 2-18**

1. What are the speakers mainly discussing?

(A) Applying for a student loan
(B) Applying for a job
(C) Applying for a scholarship
(D) Applying for accommodation

2. When do students normally apply for jobs with the Student Center?

(A) Winter
(C) Summer
(B) Spring
(D) Fall

3. Why does the man discuss his scholarship?

(A) To show that he is a good student
(B) To complain that it is inadequate
(C) To demonstrate his ability to do the job
(D) To explain why he is late in applying for work

4. Based on the information in the conversation, what will be the likely outcome?

(A) The man will get the job.
(B) The man will get a scholarship.
(C) The man will pass the training.
(D) The man will drop out of school.

[07] Conversation

Getting Ready to Listen

A. Learn the words.

Key Vocabulary

apologize	to say you are sorry
switch	to change; to shift; to exchange
full-time	fulfilling the full amount of time required or offered
drop a class	to remove oneself from a class permanently

TOEFL Vocabulary

register	to sign up for something
open enrollment	when a student is able to enroll in a course regardless of qualifications
enroll	to sign up for a program
administration	the staff of an institution or organization that deals with the business or administrative tasks
guarantee	a promise that assures a particular outcome

B. Learn the question type.

TOEFL Question Type

Main Idea

What are the speakers mainly discussing?

Why does the student visit the professor/librarian/etc?

Why does the professor ask to see the student?

- "Why" main idea questions are more commonly asked regarding conversations.
- Refer to your notes and look for the main problem the student is trying to solve.

Practice

A. Listen to the first part of the conversation and choose the correct answers.
Track 2-19

1. What is the main topic of this conversation?

    (A) A student wanting to pay for classes

    (B) A student wanting to withdraw from classes and receive a refund

2. How does the student explain the problem?

    (A) By explaining how much she owes for tuition

    (B) By explaining what she needs to do and showing the bill

Note-taking

B. Listen to the full conversation and take notes. Track 2-20

Woman - Student	Man - University Employee
• Needs to _____ • Wondering if there is open _____ _____ _____ _____ _____ _____ _____	• Asks if student is registered in _____ _____ • Half of the tuition is _____ _____ _____ _____ _____ _____

C. Choose the correct answers.

1. What is the main idea of the conversation?

(A) Directing a student how to receive a refund after dropping a class

(B) Directing a student how to pay for classes after registering

2. What is the likely outcome of dropping a class after the first two weeks?

(A) The student will not receive a full refund.

(B) The student will pay double the amount.

3. What is the problem the student has?

(A) The student needs to pay for classes.

(B) The student needs help organizing his schedule.

TOEFL Vocabulary Practice

D. Fill in the blanks with the correct words.

register	open enrollment	enroll	administration	guarantee

1. Customers are often directed to the _____ office to take care of their complaints and to receive refunds.

2. Participants for an annual bike race were told to _____ at a local bike shop.

3. Many computer shops have a lifetime _____ on some of the computer equipment they sell.

4. There is _____ for most beginners painting classes.

5. Most students _____ for classes a few months in advance.

Test

Listen to the conversation and take notes. Track 2-21

Woman - University Employee	Man - Student
• Asks the reason for _____ _____ _____ _____ _____ _____ _____ _____ _____	• Class is not what he _____ • Wants to receive a _____ • Spoke to Derrick at _____ _____ _____ _____ _____ _____ _____

Choose the correct answers. Track 2-22

1. What is the employee's attitude toward the student?

(A) She is angry.
(B) She is disappointed.
(C) She is concerned.
(D) She is frustrated.

2. What can be inferred about the employee?

(A) She cares about the student's college career.
(B) She doesn't care about the student.
(C) She wants to make sure he pays his tuition.
(D) She wants the student to be in weight training because it's a great class.

3. What problem is the student having?

(A) He dislikes the art history class he enrolled in and wants to take it next semester with a different professor.
(B) He dislikes the art history class he enrolled in and wants a refund.
(C) The art history class he enrolled in doesn't fit into his schedule.
(D) The art history class he enrolled in is too hard.

4. According to the employee, why should the student enroll in weight training?

(A) It is a fun class.
(B) It is inexpensive.
(C) It has open enrollment.
(D) It is only once a week.

Lecture - Literature

Getting Ready to Listen

A. Learn the words.

Key Vocabulary

expect	to think something will happen
biography	a book about someone's life written by someone else
sibling	a brother or sister
humor	something or someone that is funny or amusing

TOEFL Vocabulary

request	to ask for something
general	over viewing; not specific
reveal	to show or tell about something previously unknown
sophisticated	knowing a lot about the world; advanced
intelligent	clever

B. Learn the question type.

TOEFL Question Type

Main Idea

What aspect of X does the professor mainly discuss?
What is the lecture mainly about?

- The answer will be the choice that best reflects what the professor's aim is (e.g., introduce a new topic, expand on a previously discussed issue) or what he or she is mainly talking about.
- Refer to your notes and look for repeated content words or phrases.

Practice

Track 2-23

A. Listen to the first part of the lecture and choose the correct answers.

1. What is the main topic of this lecture?

   (A) Jane Austen's books   (B) Jane Austen's life

2. What are the key points in this lecture?

   (A) Jane Austen's early, middle, and later life
   (B) Her biography and books.

3. How does the professor describe the main topic?

   (A) By dividing it into parts and giving details
   (B) By discussing problems and their solutions

4. Choose the best note-taking diagram for this lecture.

   (A) Venn Diagram   (B) Problem and Solution   (C) Concept Defining
                                  Diagram   Diagram

Note-taking

B. Draw the diagram chosen in question 4. Then insert the information from questions 1 and 2.

Track 2-24

C. Now listen to the full lecture and complete your notes.

D. Choose the correct answers.

1. What is the lecture mainly about?

(A) Jane Austen's novels   (B) Jane Austen's whole life

2. What is the main point of the lecture?

(A) To show how her life played a part in her writing

(B) To give students some general information about the writer

3. Indicate whether each of the following is mentioned in the lecture.

	Yes	No
Austen married Lefroy.		
It took two years to write *Pride and Prejudice*.		
She died in 1816.		
She lived until she was forty-two years old.		

TOEFL Vocabulary Practice

E. Fill in the blanks with the correct words.

general	intelligent	sophisticated	request	reveal

1. Dolphins are very _____ animals.

2. Scientists hope that new studies will _____ the secrets of the Egyptian tombs.

3. Parents sometimes _____ a conference with their children's teachers.

4. Picasso was a very _____ artist.

5. A(n) _____ study of bees shows they are very hardworking insects.

Test

Listen to the lecture and take notes. **Track 2-25**

Famous Women Writers

- Emily Bronte

- George Elliot

- Virginia Woolf

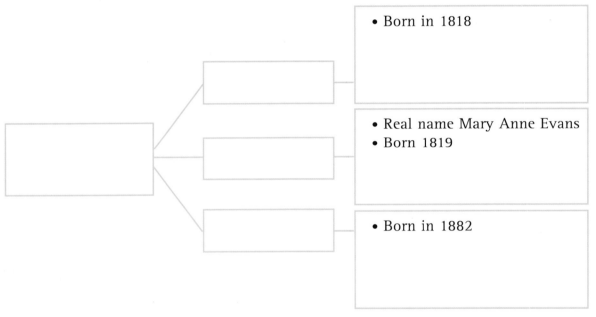

- Born in 1818

- Real name Mary Anne Evans
- Born 1819

- Born in 1882

Choose the correct answers. **Track 2-26**

1. What is the lecture mainly about?

(A) Famous novels by friends of Jane Austen
(B) The lives of three women writers who all died young
(C) The lives of three women writers who wrote famous books
(D) Women writers who wished they were men

2. What does the professor imply when she says this: 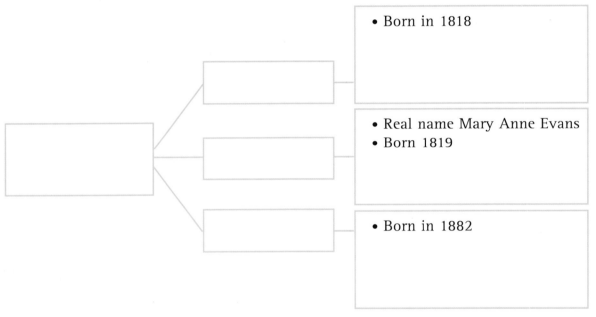 ?

(A) That Bronte's sisters' books were as sophisticated as hers
(B) That she is uncertain about whether Charlotte or Anne wrote novels
(C) That she likes Charlotte and Anne's novels more than he likes Emily's novels
(D) That being a sophisticated writer is very difficult

3. According to the professor, why did Mary Anne Evans write under a man's name?

    (A) Because she wanted to be like her hero, Emily Bronte

    (B) Because people thought women were not intelligent enough to write well

    (C) Because her novel, *Middlemarch*, revealed secrets about life in her small town

    (D) Because she thought she was not intelligent enough to be a writer

4. What is the professor's opinion of Virginia Woolf's novel?

    (A) She thinks they were all like George Eliot's novels.

    (B) She thinks they were all about war.

    (C) She thinks they are sad because the writer was a sad woman.

    (D) She believes her books were not good so she killed herself.

5. How are the points about these three writers organized?

    (A) In the order of the most famous to the least famous

    (B) In the order of writer that lived most long ago to most recently

    (C) In order of the writer who died youngest to the one who died oldest

    (D) In order of least sophisticated to most sophisticated writer

6. Indicate whether each of the following is mentioned in the lecture.

	Yes	No
Birth and death year of each writer		
Their most famous novel		
Whether writer was married or unmarried		
How each of these writers died		

Check-up

A. Choose the correct answers.

1. When answering a conversation main idea question

   (A) choose the answer that best describes the central problem of the student
   (B) refer to your notes for minor details mentioned by one of the speakers
   (C) choose the answer that best explains the speakers' emotions about the topic
   (D) listen carefully to the words and phrases spoken just before and after a repeated comment

2. What should you do when answering a lecture main idea question?

   (A) Refer to your notes for the professor's reaction to advice.
   (B) Choose the answer that best expresses what the professor is mostly talking about.
   (C) Refer to your notes for the steps in the process being described by the speaker.
   (D) Choose the answer that best represents the pattern to which the points of the lecture are presented.

Key Vocabulary Practice

B. Fill in the blanks with the correct words.

| biographies | apologize | full-time | humor |
| drop a class | siblings | expect | switch |

1. Managers often _____ to their customers when there are problems in the store.

2. Comedies are plays or films with a lot of _____.

3. In large families, _____ often compete with one another.

4. Students usually do not have enough time for _____ jobs.

5. The USA did not _____ Japan to attack them in 1941.

6. There are many good _____ of President John F. Kennedy.

7. An advisor often encourages students to _____ within the first few weeks of school, if they are uncertain about being able to pass the class.

8. Participants in a triathlon _____ from swimming to biking, and finally to running.

[08] Conversation

Getting Ready to Listen

A. Learn the words.

Key Vocabulary

details	personal facts about someone, like their name and address
settle in	to adapt to a new environment
issue	something for discussion or of general concern
forward	to redirect mail or information to a new location

TOEFL Vocabulary

abroad	referring to another country or other countries
option	a choice that can be made
partnership	the relationship between two or more people or organizations involved in the same activity
exchange	an arrangement between schools or organizations for stays in each other's schools or organizations
immigration	the control point at an airport or border crossing where people must stop to have their passports officially checked

B. Learn the question type.

TOEFL Question Type

Detail

According to the man/woman, what is the main problem with X?

What does the man suggest the woman do?

- Refer to your notes for important details; the test will not ask for minor details.
- Select the answer choice most consistent with the speaker's relationship to the main problem of the conversation.

Practice

A. Listen to the first part of the conversation and choose the correct answers.

Track 2-27

1. What is the main topic of this conversation?

   (A) A student from abroad arriving at the university

   (B) A student thinking of going abroad for a semester

2. How does the university worker explain what options are available?

   (A) She explains that there are many possibilities and asks if he has any preferences.

   (B) She lists the possible countries that he could study in.

Note-taking

B. Listen to the full conversation and take notes. Track 2-28

Man - Student	Woman - University Employee
• About to finish the first year of _____ _____ • Is considering studying _____ _____ _____ _____ _____ _____ _____	• Has a few _____ • University has partnerships and _____ _____ _____ _____ _____ _____ _____ _____ _____ _____

C. Choose the correct answers.

1. Why is the student talking to the university worker?

(A) To find out what countries the university has partnerships with

(B) To get advice on what options are available to him for studying abroad

2. According to the University worker, what enables students to settle in more easily abroad?

(A) Knowing the language   (B) Having family in the country

3. According to the student, why would the school in Paris be perfect for him?

(A) He has family in France.   (B) He has always wanted to live in Paris.

TOEFL Vocabulary Practice

D. Fill in the blanks with the correct words.

abroad	option	partnership	exchange	immigration

1. If you would like to buy a car, you should look at more than one _____.

2. When you arrive at an airport in another country, you must pass through _____.

3. In the summertime, many people like to go _____ for their vacation.

4. Many schools have a(n) _____ program with other schools around the world.

5. When two people want to go into business together, they will form a(n) _____.

Test

Listen to the conversation and take notes. **Track 2-29**

Woman - Student	Man - University Employee
• Is a student from _____ • Arrived last semester and _____ _____ • Is an _____ _____ _____ _____ _____ _____	• Is here to help _____ _____ _____ • Can change classes _____ _____ _____ _____ _____ _____

Choose the correct answers. **Track 2-30**

1. Why is the woman talking to the university worker?
   (A) To explain that she is a foreign student and would like some help
   (B) To tell the university worker that she does not know what form she has to complete for immigration
   (C) To get some advice for settling into a new country more easily
   (D) To inform the university that she has recently arrived in the country

2. According to the student, what is the problem that she is facing at the university?
   (A) She cannot read English.
   (B) She is having difficulty making friends and meeting people.
   (C) She misses home.
   (D) She is having difficulty with the language.

3. How does the student organize the information about what she would like from the university?
   (A) She explains that she is a foreign student and then asks for help with an immigration problem.
   (B) She asks for help with an immigration form and then for assistance with her studies.
   (C) She explains that she is a foreign student and asks for help with her studies and then about an immigration form that she requires.
   (D) She asks for help with her studies, then for help getting an immigration form, and then reveals that she is a foreign student.

4. Why does the student say this: ◯ ?
   (A) To emphasize to the university worker that she is a student from abroad
   (B) To support the notion that she is new to the country
   (C) To get the university worker to help her
   (D) To explain that she can speak Spanish

Lecture - Environment

Getting Ready to Listen

A. Learn the words.

Key Vocabulary

reuse	to use something again
fair	unbiased; unprejudiced
pass	to approve
strict	enforcing rules

TOEFL Vocabulary

adjust	to change slightly
initiate	to start something
aware	knowing something
globe	the Earth or the world
legislate	to make laws

B. Learn the question type.

TOEFL Question Type

Detail

According to the professor, what is one way that X can affect Y?

What resulted from X?

- The correct answer will usually be consistent with the main idea/topic of the lecture.
- Refer to your notes and look for key words written under main idea headings.

Practice

A. **Listen to the first part of the lecture and choose the correct answers.** `Track 2-31`

1. What is the main topic of this lecture?

   (A) How to help the environment   (B) How to use less

2. What are the key points of this lecture?

   (A) How both one person and communities can help the environment
   (B) How to become aware of the environment

3. How does the professor describe the main topic?

   (A) He talks about the effect of people on the environment.
   (B) He talks about the similarities and differences in how people and communities can help the environment.

4. Choose the best note-taking diagram for this lecture.

   (A) Problem and Solution   (B) Venn Diagram   (C) Categorizing
       Diagram   Diagram

Note-taking

B. **Draw the diagram chosen in question 4. Then insert the information from questions 1 and 2.**

C. **Now listen to the full lecture and complete your notes.** `Track 2-32`

D. Choose the correct answers.

1. What is the lecture mainly about?

    (A) Things that people and communities can do to help the environment.

    (B) How to keep the globe clean.

2. According to the professor, what will a tax on people who use too much energy do?

    (A) Make them use less and punish people who hurt the environment

    (B) Make them aware of how much they use and make them use less

3. According to the professor, which of the following is NOT an easy way for one person to help?

    (A) Initiate projects that make people aware of the environment.

    (B) Pay lots of taxes.

TOEFL Vocabulary Practice

E. Fill in the blanks with the correct words.

adjust	initiate	aware	globe	legislate

1. Governments _____ new rules to keep the people safe and happy.

2. People have to _____ their clothing choice depending on the weather.

3. Children are often not _____ of how dangerous drugs can be.

4. Countries around the _____ are all doing things to stop climate change.

5. One person with a good idea can often _____ change in a community.

Test

Listen to the lecture and take notes. **Track 2-33**

How America and Europe Help the Environment

- Taxes on gas

- Strict laws on smoke

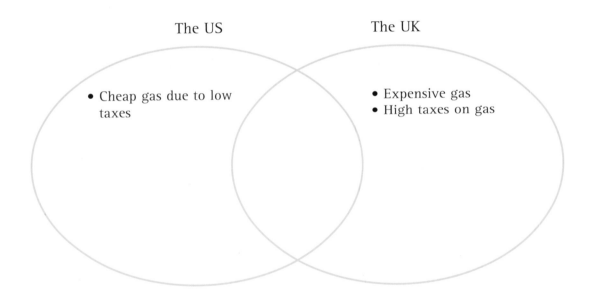

The US

- Cheap gas due to low taxes

The UK

- Expensive gas
- High taxes on gas

Choose the correct answers. **Track 2-34**

1. What is the main idea of the lecture?

    (A) Similarities and differences in gas prices in the US and the UK

    (B) Similarities and differences in smoke laws in the US and the UK

    (C) Similarities and differences in punishing polluters in the US and the UK

    (D) Similarities and differences in how the US and the UK legislate to help the environment

2. According to the professor, what is an easy way to see how taxes affect the US and the UK?

(A) Moving to the US
(B) Moving to the UK
(C) Going to the gas station
(D) Adjusting the amount that you use

3. Why does the professor say this: ◯ ?

(A) To make the student feel bad
(B) To give the student an idea of a community she can easily understand
(C) To confuse the student
(D) To show how easy his lectures are to understand

4. Why does the professor discuss gas prices in the US and the UK?
(A) To give an easy example of how the two try to limit the use of gas
(B) To show that the UK is much more expensive
(C) To show that the UK helps the environment more
(D) To show that the US has much cheaper gas

5. What is the professor's attitude toward smoke laws in the US?
(A) He thinks that they are good enough.
(B) He is glad to see that they are becoming stricter.
(C) He thinks they should be punished.
(D) He thinks that smoke laws there do not work.

6. What is the likely outcome of the US having stricter smoke laws?
(A) People won't be punished as often.
(B) Taxes will be much higher.
(C) It will help the environment.
(D) Europe will initiate even stricter laws on smoke in the air.

Check-up

A. Choose the correct answers.

1. When answering a conversation detail question
   (A) select the answer that explains the speaker's attitude toward the problem
   (B) choose the answer that includes one of the major details from your notes
   (C) select the answer that best explains an idiom or expression used by the speakers
   (D) choose the answer that explains why a speaker asks a certain question

2. What should you do when answering a lecture detail question?
   (A) Choose the answer that best summarizes the professor's aim for giving the lecture.
   (B) Select an answer that includes information that can be inferred from the professor's attitude.
   (C) Choose a detail that is mentioned in the lecture and is consistent with the main idea of the lecture.
   (D) Select the answer that best represents the pattern to which the points of the lecture are presented.

Key Vocabulary Practice

B. Fill in the blanks with the correct words.

reuse	fair	passes	strict
details	settle in	issues	forward

1. When people move houses, they should _____ their mail to the new address.

2. In the workplace, workers can have meetings to discuss any _____ they may have.

3. A teacher must be _____ when testing students so that everybody has an equal chance to succeed.

4. When children move to a new school, they can find it difficult to _____ and make friends.

5. Parents are often _____ with their teenage children.

6. A government _____ laws in order to try and solve problems in their country.

7. When posting a letter, you must write the _____ of the person you are writing to on the front of the envelope.

8. A good way to _____ a Coke bottle is as a water bottle.

[09] Conversation

Getting Ready to Listen

A. Learn the words.

Key Vocabulary

congratulations	a term used to say well done and to give your best wishes
a number of	numerous; many
praise	to commend something and speak highly of it
review	to critique or evaluate

TOEFL Vocabulary

advice	an opinion given about what should be done in a situation
ambition	when someone has goals, dreams, or desire that they want to achieve
interpretation	the way somebody understands or explains something according to their own opinion
contemplate	to think about a decision or action
convince	to persuade or win over someone's belief or beliefs

B. Learn the question type.

TOEFL Question Type

Function

What can be inferred from the man/woman's response?

What is the purpose of the man/woman's response?

Why does the man/woman say this: 🎧 ?

You will often hear part of the conversation again.

• The question may focus on an idiom or expression that the speaker uses, so focus on understanding the informal language used.

• In conversations, speakers often ask questions to emphasize an emotion or to check another speaker's understanding.

Practice

A. Listen to the first part of the conversation and choose the correct answers.
    `Track 2-35`

1. What is the main topic of this conversation?
    (A) The student is telling the professor that he does not want to enter the essay competition.
    (B) The student would like some advice from the professor on what to write about.

2. How does the student explain his situation?
    (A) He explains that he would like the professor's advice and then gives details of the competition and his problem.
    (B) He describes the competition and then asks the professor to help him choose a subject to write about.

Note-taking

B. Listen to the full conversation and take notes.   `Track 2-36`

Man - Student	Woman - Professor
• Invited to _____ _____ • Is not sure what _____ • Must write about something that he likes and _____	• Congratulates _____ _____ • A number of teachers have _____ _____

C. Choose the correct answers.

1. Why does the professor say this: ◯ ? `Track 2-37`

   (A) Because she believes that the student enjoys writing about books

   (B) Because the student is especially good at writing essays about books

2. What does the student imply when he says this: ◯ ? `Track 2-38`

   (A) That he has an idea what he would like to do and would like to be reassured about it

   (B) That he does not really believe that it is the best option

3. According to the student, what is the main problem that he is having in choosing an essay topic?

   (A) He cannot think of anything that he wants to write about.

   (B) There are so many options that he does not know what would be the best one.

TOEFL Vocabulary Practice

D. Fill in the blanks with the correct words.

advice	interpretation	ambition	contemplate	convince

1. When looking at a painting, people will make their own _____ of what it is about.

2. When making an important decision, people often ask for _____ from somebody they trust.

3. When you have a job interview, you must _____ the interviewer that you would be good for the job.

4. When people are young, they often have at least one _____ about what they want from life.

5. When facing a decision, people should _____ what would be the best choice for them.

Test

🎧 Listen to the conversation and take notes.   `Track 2-39`

Woman - Student	Man - Professor
• Has been asked to show _____ _____ • Is has been an _____ _____ _____ • Has had a lot of praise from _____ _____ _____ _____ _____ _____ _____	• Has seen _____ • Is convinced _____ _____ _____ • Everybody's interpretation _____ _____ _____ _____ _____ _____ _____ _____

Choose the correct answers.   `Track 2-40`

1. What problem does the student have?
   (A) She has been asked to show her work at an exhibition, but does not know what paintings to exhibit.
   (B) She is scared of the teacher's opinion of her work.
   (C) She has been asked to exhibit her art work in a university art show but is nervous about it.
   (D) She would like to be able to control what people think about her art.

2. According to the professor, which of the following is false?
   (A) That everyone will love her work
   (B) That the student can control what people see in her work
   (C) That everyone's interpretation of art is different
   (D) You just have to do your best

3. What does the student mean when she says this: 🎧 ?
   (A) She is worried that the teachers and professionals will not understand or like her work.
   (B) She is worried that they will not agree on the meaning of her work.
   (C) She is nervous about speaking to art professionals.
   (D) She is worried that very few teachers and professionals will come to see her work.

4. According to the professor, what is the likely outcome of the exhibition?
   (A) The teachers and professionals will argue over her work.
   (B) That teachers will praise her artwork.
   (C) That everybody at the exhibition will agree on the meaning of her art.
   (D) Everybody will love her work.

Lecture - Health

Getting Ready to Listen

A. Learn the words.

Key Vocabulary

symptom	a sign of an illness
quantity	amount
gym	a place where people can exercise inside
alert	mentally lively

TOEFL Vocabulary

minimal	smallest possible
equate	to cause the equivalent of something
implementation	the starting or carrying out of a plan
output	production
exclude	to keep someone or something out

B. Learn the question type.

TOEFL Question Type

Function

What can be inferred from the professor/student's response?

What is the purpose of the professor/student's response?

Why does the professor say this: 🎧 ?

You will often hear part of the lecture again.

- In lectures, speakers often ask rhetorical questions to emphasize a point or check the students' understanding.
- In lectures, speakers often tell stories to give examples or to describe a process.
- Refer to your notes to see how the speaker's words best relate to the main idea of the lecture.

Practice

A. Listen to the first part of the lecture and choose the correct answers. `Track 2-41`

1. What is the main topic of this lecture?

   (A) Changes to make you study better   (B) How to be more awake

2. What are the key points in this lecture?

   (A) People have many problems with their brain.

   (B) Changing your diet, sleeping patterns, and exercise can help you study better.

3. How does the professor describe the main topic?

   (A) He talks about problem areas and then offers suggestions to improve them.

   (B) He talks about all the different things you must do to improve your studying.

4. Choose the best note-taking diagram for this lecture.

   (A) Concept Defining   (B) Venn Diagram   (C) Problem and Solution
       Diagram   Diagram

Note-taking

B. Draw the diagram chosen in question 4. Then insert the information from questions 1 and 2.

C. Now listen to the full lecture and complete your notes. `Track 2-42`

D. Choose the correct answers.

1. Why does the professor say this: ( )? **Track 2-43**

(A) He wants everyone to know what the brain does.

(B) He wants to emphasize how busy the brain is.

(C) He wants people to use their brain less.

(D) He wants people to study harder.

2. According to the professor, why can it be difficult to start your work?

(A) You need to go to the gym.

(B) You must change your diet.

(C) You need to sleep more.

(D) You have a lot of energy.

3. Why does the professor say this: ( )? **Track 2-44**

(A) He wants to make people feel badly.

(B) He wants to give an example for how each student can study harder.

(C) He doesn't think that the students study hard.

(D) He thinks that it is important.

TOEFL Vocabulary Practice

E. Fill in the blanks with the correct words.

minimal	equates	implementation	output	excluded

1. Poor people often get _____ amounts of money at their jobs.

2. Factories help people increase the _____ of things that they make.

3. Before Jackie Robinson, American baseball _____ African Americans.

4. The _____ of a gym routine can help people lose weight and feel much better.

5. Studying hard often _____ to better grades on tests.

Test

Listen to the lecture and take notes. Track 2-45

A balanced lifestyle

- Make time for friends and games
- Go to the gym
- Have fun
- Spend time with family

Problem	Solution
Feel bad	
• Friend plays computers all day, doesn't want _____ _____	
• Good student, always studies, but _____ _____	
• Workers were not happy, didn't _____	

Choose the correct answers. Track 2-46

1. What is the main idea of the lecture?

(A) How to keep from being sick
(B) How to be happy at work
(C) The importance of a balanced lifestyle
(D) The importance of working hard

2. What is the professor's opinion of people who study all the time?

    (A) They are always right.

    (B) Other people should be more like them.

    (C) She doesn't like them.

    (D) While studying is good, it is important to do other things as well.

3. Why does the professor discuss balanced lifestyles in companies?

    (A) To show that rich people have balanced lifestyles

    (B) To show that it is useful in the real world

    (C) To show that only adults are smart enough to have a balanced lifestyle

    (D) To show that it is important to have a balanced lifestyle to get a job

4. Why does the professor say this: 🎧 ?

    (A) The professor wants people to make enough time for lots of things.

    (B) It is very tiring to do the same thing all the time.

    (C) Studying can make you sick.

    (D) The professor doesn't want people to waste their energy.

5. According to the professor, what happened to workers who spent minimal amounts of time with their family?

    (A) They were really tired.

    (B) They hated to go to work.

    (C) They were more alert.

    (D) They were not happy.

6. According to the professor, what is the likely outcome of having a balanced lifestyle?

    (A) You can feel happy and fulfilled.

    (B) You will be in very good shape.

    (C) You won't be sick.

    (D) You will be very smart.

Check-up

A. Choose the correct answers.

1. When answering a conversation function question
   (A) refer to your notes for any strong emotions expressed by the speakers
   (B) check your notes for the main problem the student needs to solve
   (C) refer to your notes to see if any questions were asked to emphasize a point or to check understanding
   (D) check your notes for any strong opinions mentioned by the speakers

2. What should you do when answering a lecture function question?
   (A) Select the answer that best contradicts the main idea of the lecture.
   (B) Pick the answer that best explains why the professor asks a rhetorical question.
   (C) Select the answer that includes the most minor details from the lecture.
   (D) Pick the answer that most logically suggests what the professor will discuss next.

Key Vocabulary Practice

B. Fill in the blanks with the correct words.

review	symptom	praise	quantities
a number of	gym	alert	congratulations

1. If you are skilled at something, you will often receive a lot of _____ for it from people.

2. People who go to the _____ every day often get much stronger.

3. Before watching a movie, people will often read a(n) _____ on it to see if the movie is good or not.

4. Policemen always need to be _____ of what is happening around them.

5. If you have more than one favorite hobby, it is common to say that you have _____ them.

6. It is often cheaper to buy things in large _____.

7. One _____ of the flu is a really bad headache.

8. When somebody wins a competition of some kind, it is common to wish him or her _____.

[10] Conversation

Getting Ready to Listen

A. Learn the words.

Key Vocabulary

misplace	to lose or be unable to find something
anytime	at any moment in time
careless	without care; irresponsible
replacement	a substitute for something

TOEFL Vocabulary

database	a file or record containing information
undergraduate	a scholar or student doing a Bachelor's degree
declare	to pronounce or state something
indicate	to point out or show something
term	a set period of time during an academic year

B. Learn the question type.

TOEFL Question Type

Attitude

What is the man/woman's opinion of X?

What can be inferred about the student?

- Take notes of any strong emotions or opinions mentioned by the speakers.
- Pay attention to tone of the speakers' voices as they respond to each other.

Practice

 A. Listen to the first part of the conversation and choose the correct answers.

Track 3-1

1. What is the main topic of this conversation?

(A) A student has lost his identification card and would like some help.

(B) A student has lost two identification cards in one month.

2. How does the student explain his situation?

(A) He explains that he has lost his ID card and asks what he needs to do next.

(B) He describes what kind of ID card he has lost and explains that he would like to buy another one.

Note-taking

B. Listen to the full conversation and take notes. Track 3-2

Man - Student	Woman - University Employee
• Has lost _____	• Needs the student's _____
• Cannot remember _____	• Lots of students lose _____
	• Details indicate that _____

C. Choose the correct answers.

1. What is the university worker's opinion of the student when she finds out that he has lost two ID cards?

   (A) She is frustrated by the student's carelessness with his ID cards.
   (B) She is hopeful that he will not lose a third ID card.

2. What is the student's attitude toward the university worker at the student affairs office?

   (A) He does not care that he is causing an inconvenience and just wants a new ID card.
   (B) He is sorry for the trouble he has caused and realizes that he has been careless.

3. What does the student mean when he says this: ⌢? **Track 3-3**

   (A) That he is a normally a careful person and has just had some bad luck with his last two ID cards
   (B) That he is careless and does not look after his student cards properly

TOEFL Vocabulary Practice

D. Fill in the blanks with the correct words.

undergraduate	declares	indicate	database	term

1. Many students that study far from home live on campus during the school _____.

2. Universities keep their students' information and details in a computer _____.

3. When somebody starts their first year at university, they become a(n) _____.

4. When somebody _____ something, they state it officially.

5. When driving a car, people _____ that they will turn a corner using a flashing light.

Test

Listen to the conversation and take notes. **Track 3-4**

Woman - Student	Man - University Employee
• Is a _____ _____	• Would like to know _____ _____
• Would like a _____ _____	• Must declare _____ _____
• Still has _____ _____ _____ _____ _____ _____ _____ _____	• Asks if there is _____ _____ _____ _____ _____ _____ _____ _____

Choose the correct answers. **Track 3-5**

1. Why is the student talking to the university worker?
   (A) She has lost her student ID card and would like a replacement one.
   (B) She is a new undergraduate and would like to register for her first student ID card.
   (C) She would like to change her address and details on her current ID card.
   (D) She would like a replacement card to change the photograph on her current one.

2. According to the university worker, what is the reason that the student may not have a replacement card?
   (A) Once photographs are placed in the university database, they cannot be changed.
   (B) Replacements can only be issued if a card has been declared lost, damaged, or stolen.
   (C) The student's current card is too old to be replaced.
   (D) The student is too close to graduating to receive a replacement card.

3. What is the student's opinion of her current student ID card?
   (A) She is frustrated that her old photograph does not look like her anymore and is not nice.
   (B) She is angry that the card is old and faded and that it does not look good.
   (C) She is happy that she has had it for so long and would like another copy of it.
   (D) She is anxious that she will lose it and would like an extra copy in case she does.

4. How is the conversation organized?
   (A) The student asks for a new card before giving her reasons for wanting one.
   (B) The student explains the reasons for her dislike of her current card and then asks for a new one.
   (C) The student gives an example of why she dislikes her current card and then requests a new one.
   (D) The student supports the policy against giving out replacement cards at will but then requests one regardless.

Lecture - Technology

Getting Ready to Listen

A. Learn the words.

Key Vocabulary

electronics	devices that work electronically
self-reliance	the state of not depending on others
durable	strong; long lasting; not prone to wear
thrive	to do very well

TOEFL Vocabulary

predominantly	mainly; consisting mostly of
innovation	the process of creating or inventing
phase	a time period in a sequence of events
competitive	the quality of trying to outperform others
commission	to pay someone to build or create something

B. Learn the question type.

TOEFL Question Type

Attitude

What can be inferred from the professor/student response?

What does the professor mean when he/she says this: ⟨🎧⟩?

- Some questions will replay part of the lecture again.
- Pay attention to the words and phrases spoken just before and after a repeated comment to understand its context.

Practice

A. Listen to the first part of the lecture and choose the correct answers. Track 3-6

1. What is the main topic of this lecture?

   (A) The secrets to Sony's success   (B) The importance of innovation

2. What are the key points of this lecture?

   (A) Sony succeeded because they had enough startup capital, experienced workers, and ambition.
   (B) Sony succeeded because of innovation, listening to the consumer, and self-reliance.

3. How does the professor describe the main topic?

   (A) By showing the cause and effect of certain actions
   (B) By discussing each factor in turn

4. Choose the best note-taking diagram for this lecture.

   (A) Categorizing Diagram   (B) Cause and Effect   (C) Problem and Solution
                                      Diagram   Diagram

| Note-taking |

B. Draw the diagram chosen in question 4. Then insert the information from questions 1 and 2.

C. Now listen to the full lecture and complete your notes. Track 3-7

D. Choose the correct answers.

1. What is the professor's opinion of Sony products?

(A) He thinks they are inferior.
(B) He thinks they are too expensive.
(C) He thinks they are high quality.
(D) He thinks they are too small.

2. What is the professor's attitude toward Sony?

(A) He thinks they have unfair business practices.
(B) He thinks they cut corners, which reduces quality.
(C) He thinks their success is due to their business practices.
(D) He thinks their success is not well deserved.

3. Why does the professor say this: 🎧 ? `Track 3-8`
(A) To warn students against leaking industry secrets
(B) To demonstrate the importance of worker loyalty
(C) To explain why some companies give up early
(D) To show why it is important to be constantly improving

TOEFL Vocabulary Practice

E. Fill in the blanks with the correct words.

predominantly	innovation	phase	competitive	commission

1. Students in nursing programs are _____ female.

2. One can _____ an architect to design his or her dream house.

3. A company that comes out with new and better products every year demonstrates good _____.

4. Planning is just the first _____ in creating a new product.

5. A(n) _____ company will always try to make a better product than other companies make.

Test

Listen to the lecture and take notes. `Track 3-9`

Car Making in Japan

- Pre-war
- World War II
- Post-war

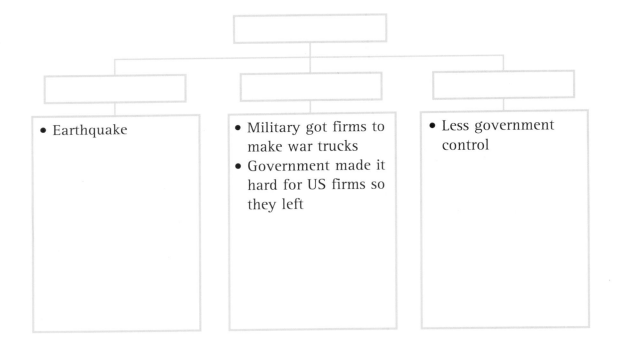

- Earthquake

- Military got firms to make war trucks
- Government made it hard for US firms so they left

- Less government control

Choose the correct answers. `Track 3-10`

1. What is the lecture mainly about?

    (A) The impact of World War II on Japan

    (B) The Japanese car industry

    (C) How the Japanese government helped the car industry

    (D) How the Japanese government hindered the car industry

2. According to the lecture, why did the American firms leave Japan?

    (A) Because the government took away their license to do business
    (B) Because government rules made it difficult to compete
    (C) Because they were on different sides of World War II
    (D) Because they hadn't made any profits in Japan

3. What is the professor's attitude toward Japanese cars?

    (A) He thinks they are the fastest in the world.
    (B) He thinks they are the most expensive in the world.
    (C) He thinks they are the most stylish in the world.
    (D) He thinks they are the most durable in the world.

4. Listen again to part of the lecture. Then answer the question.

Why does the professor say this: ?

    (A) To give an example of a country with a large car industry
    (B) To emphasize his point that the best cars are Japanese
    (C) To demonstrate the importance of the talk
    (D) To show how dependent Japan is on its car industry

5. How did the professor organize the lecture?

    (A) By discussing three phases in turn
    (B) By comparing and contrasting different phases
    (C) By showing cause and effect relationships for each event
    (D) By presenting a problem and explaining the solution

6. Choose whether each of the following helped or hindered the Japanese car industry.

	Helped	Hindered
Earthquake		
Military		
Government		
US car firms		

Check-up

A. Choose the correct answers.

1. When answering a conversation attitude question

    (A) listen to the tone of the speakers' voices to understand their attitude

    (B) listen for the sequence of steps to understand the speakers' emotions

    (C) listen to the volume of the speakers' voices to understand the main idea

    (D) listen for repeated content words or phrases to understand the speakers' purpose

2. What should you do when answering a lecture attitude question?

    (A) Look in your notes for repeated content words or phrases to give you a clue about the main idea.

    (B) Choose the answer that puts the steps of a sequence into the correct order.

    (C) Look at your notes for any pattern to how the points of the lecture were presented.

    (D) Choose the answer that is most consistent with the professor's tone of voice.

Key Vocabulary Practice

B. Fill in the blanks with the correct words.

electronics	misplace	self-reliance	anytime
durable	careless	thrive	replacement

1. A(n) _____ store sells TVs, radios, and other appliances that plug into the wall.

2. If a shop is open all day and night, someone can buy items from it _____.

3. Students need to have _____ when they move to a university away from home.

4. If someone loses a bankcard or passport, it is important to cancel it and ask for a(n) _____ one.

5. In winter, it is best to have a(n) _____ coat for the harsh weather.

6. When someone repeatedly loses their possessions, they could be said to be _____.

7. When people _____ their car keys, they cannot remember where they last put them.

8. Children often _____ in a positive environment.

[11] Conversation

Getting Ready to Listen

A. Learn the words.

Key Vocabulary

IT	information technology: any kind of technology, such as computers, which enable electronic communication and can hold electronic information
laptop	a small, portable computer that can be folded in two and can be used on and placed on its user's lap
virus	a computer program that can cause computers to break down or malfunction
install	to add something

TOEFL Vocabulary

assignment	a task or mission given to a select person or people
file	a folder on a computer's memory that contains documents of information
defend	to guard something or someone from attack; to keep something safe
resistant	difficult or impossible to change or affect
task	an act that has to be carried out or done

B. Learn the question type.

TOEFL Question Type

Organization

How is the discussion organized?

Why does the man/woman discuss X?

Why does the man/woman mention X?

• Organization questions are more commonly asked after lectures rather than conversations.

• Refer to your notes for any connections between parts of the conversation.

Practice

A. Listen to the first part of the conversation and choose the correct answers.

Track 3-11

1. What is the main topic of this conversation?

    (A) The student's laptop computer is not working properly and he would like the IT center to repair it.

    (B) The student would like to find out about how to defend his laptop computer against viruses.

2. How does the student explain his situation?

    (A) He states that his computer has a virus and asks the university worker to fix it for him.

    (B) He suggests that his computer may have a virus and explains how important the information on his computer is to him.

Note-taking

B. Listen to the full conversation and take notes. Track 3-12

Man - Student	Woman - University Employee
• Is having trouble _____ _____	• Can have a _____ _____
• Thinks that it may _____ _____ _____ _____ _____ _____ _____ _____	• Asks if the computer has _____ _____ • It is a program that _____ _____ _____ _____ _____ _____ _____

C. Choose the correct answers.

1. Why does the student discuss the assignments that he must submit and the files that he needs to do?

(A) To give an example of how busy he is at university

(B) To emphasize the importance of fixing his computer quickly and getting rid of the virus on it

2. How does the university worker organize the information about computer viruses and anti-virus programs?

(A) She asks the student if he has an anti-virus program, then explains what it is and the importance of it.

(B) She explains that she has found a virus on the computer and then describes what a virus is.

3. What does the student mean when he says this: ⌒ ? Track 3-13

(A) He is going to drop out of school.   (B) The files are very important.

TOEFL Vocabulary Practice

D. Fill in the blanks with the correct words.

assignment	file	defend	resistant	tasks

1. My neighbor has a guard dog to _____ his house.

2. At the weekend many people do household _____, like cleaning the bathroom or washing the floors.

3. When people grow up, they often become more _____ to catching colds and becoming ill.

4. When people have many documents on a computer, they will put them into a(n) _____ to make them easier to find and organize.

5. At the end of an academic year at a school or university, students often have more than one _____ to hand in.

Test

Listen to the conversation and take notes. Track 3-14

Woman - Student	Man - University Employee
• Her laptop _____ _____ • Dropped it and _____ _____ • Has a big _____ _____ _____ _____ _____ _____	• Laptops are not _____ _____ • A padded _____ _____ • When the computer is _____ _____ _____ _____ _____ _____

Choose the correct answers. Track 3-15

1. What problem does the student have?
   (A) She has an assignment and asks the university worker to help her with it.
   (B) She does not have a replacement power button for her laptop and would like one from the IT center.
   (C) Her laptop has stopped working since she dropped it and she would like the university worker to look at it for her.
   (D) Her laptop is broken and she wants to replace it.

2. According to the university worker, what is a good way to protect a laptop computer?
   (A) By carrying it in a backpack
   (B) By securing the power button and battery pack on the computer
   (C) By transporting the computer in a padded laptop bag
   (D) By always carrying it with two hands

3. What does the university worker mean when he says this: ( )?
   (A) That if a laptop computer is dropped it will often break
   (B) That laptop computers are slippery
   (C) That laptop computers are sturdy and can withstand being dropped
   (D) That laptop computers are badly made and fall apart easily

4. How does the student organize the information about what happened to her laptop?
   (A) She describes what happens when she tries to turn it on and then explains that she dropped it.
   (B) She explains that she carries her laptop in a bag, and then explains that it stopped working when it was dropped.
   (C) She explains that she has an assignment to finish and then that she has dropped her laptop and cannot complete the assignment without it.
   (D) She explains that her laptop has stopped working, that she dropped it, and then she describes how it looks after the fall.

Lecture - Civics and Government

Getting Ready to Listen

A. Learn the words.

Key Vocabulary

party	a political organization
election	a day and a time when people vote to decide on something
state	an area forming a smaller part of a country
impeach	to say that a person in the government did something illegal

TOEFL Vocabulary

straightforward	easy and not difficult to understand or do
distinguish	to set something apart and show differences between it and something else
significant	a large amount
convene	to gather for a meeting
legitimate	well reasoned or real

B. Learn the question type.

TOEFL Question Type

Organization

How does the professor organize the information about X that he/she presents to the class?
How is the discussion organized?
Why does the professor mention X?

- Organization questions are more commonly asked after lectures rather than conversations.
- Look at your notes for any pattern to how the points of the lecture were presented (e.g., from most to least important, according to time, etc.).

Practice

A. **A.** **Listen to the first part of the lecture and choose the correct answers.** `Track 3-16`

1. What is the main topic of this lecture?

    (A) A president's job   (B) How to become president

2. What are the key points of this lecture?

    (A) How a candidate declares his candidacy, and then becomes president
    (B) How to win an election

3. How does the professor describe the main topic?

    (A) The professor describes each step that a candidate must take.
    (B) The professor talks about candidates' problems and then how to solve them.

4. Choose the best note-taking diagram for this lecture.

    (A) Problem and Solution   (B) Ordering Diagram   (C) Cause and Effect
        Diagram   Diagram

Note-taking

B. Draw the diagram chosen in question 4. Then insert the information from questions 1 and 2.

C. Now listen to the full lecture and complete your notes. `Track 3-17`

D. Choose the correct answers.

1. Why does the professor talk about each candidate choosing a party before they go into an election?

(A) Candidates usually choose which party's election they want to be in.

(B) It can help them win the big election.

2. Listen again to part of the lecture. Then answer the question. 🎧 **Track 3-18**

What is the professor's opinion about the big election?

(A) He thinks people like to vote.

(B) He thinks it is expensive and takes a lot of time.

3. Why does the professor talk about the party election before the bigger election?

(A) Because the party election is first

(B) Because people are more interested in the party election

TOEFL Vocabulary Practice

E. Fill in the blanks with the correct words.

straightforward	distinguish	significant	convened	legitimate

1. Dubai is trying to _____ itself by building big, beautiful buildings everywhere.

2. Rice makes up a _____ amount of the Asian diet.

3. In 1919, the leaders of all the fighting countries _____ in France at Versailles to end World War I.

4. The rules of soccer are pretty _____: kick the ball into the goal, don't use your hands.

5. Lots of people think that gold is the one _____ form of money.

Test

Listen to the lecture and take notes. **Track 3-19**

Impeachment

- Lower house can impeach the president

- Upper house has a trial

- If over 67% vote yes, the president must quit

Impeachment

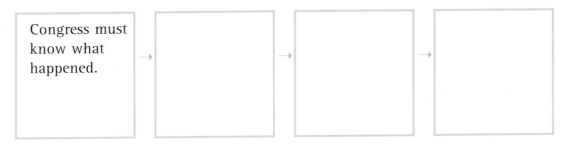

Congress must know what happened.	→		→		→	

Choose the correct answers. **Track 3-20**

1. What is the main idea of the lecture?

(A) How to become vice president
(B) How the president is impeached
(C) How the Congress finds out what happened
(D) How Congress votes to make the president quit

2. According to the professor, what happens if the lower house finds out that the president did something significant to break the law?

(A) The president is impeached.
(B) The president must quit.
(C) The vice-president becomes president.
(D) The upper house votes.

3. Listen again to part of the lecture. Then answer the question. 🎧

What is the professor's attitude toward presidents who break the law?

(A) He or she should be impeached.
(B) He or she should not have an election.
(C) People should be able to choose a new one, but they can't do that.
(D) People need to be very careful about who they choose.

4. What does the professor mean when he says this: 🎧 ?

(A) Presidents are often impeached.
(B) Everyone loves the president.
(C) Lots of things are said about the president that are not true.
(D) People should not say bad things about the president.

5. Why does the professor discuss past impeachments?

(A) To show that it does happen, even though it is rare
(B) To show that there are bad presidents
(C) To show that people usually choose good presidents
(D) To show that the process works

6. According to the professor, what is the outcome of a vote by the upper house if the vote is only twenty-five percent?

(A) The vice president must quit.
(B) The president must quit.
(C) The vice president becomes president.
(D) The president does not have to quit.

Check-up

A. Choose the correct answers.

1. When answering a conversation organization question
   (A) choose the answer that explains the main problem the students want solved
   (B) select the answer that best contradicts the main idea of the lecture
   (C) choose the answer that best explains the connection between parts of the conversation
   (D) select the answer that best explains an idiom or expression used by the speakers

2. What should you do when answering a lecture organization question?
   (A) Choose the answer that best explains the speakers' emotions about the topic.
   (B) Select the answer that includes the most minor details from the lecture.
   (C) Choose the answer that is most consistent with the professor's tone of voice.
   (D) Select the answer that best explains the pattern to how the points in the lecture were presented.

Key Vocabulary Practice

B. Fill in the blanks with the correct words.

parties	laptop	elections	virus
states	IT	install	impeached

1. The US has fifty different _____.
2. Because they are small and easy to carry, many people like to travel with a(n) _____ computer.
3. Many children learn about _____ at school so that they can write things on computers, use the Internet, and send emails.
4. When someone buys a computer game for their computer, they must _____ it onto the computer before they can play it.
5. President Bill Clinton was _____ but did not have to quit being president.
6. The US has two main political _____—the Republicans and the Democrats.
7. Some countries like North Korea and Myanmar do not have _____ for president.
8. If a computer catches a(n) _____, it can stop working correctly and be very difficult to repair.

[12] Conversation

Getting Ready to Listen

A. Learn the words.

Key Vocabulary

post	to place information where people can access it, often online
lab	a class where research or testing is carried out in a laboratory, in conjunction with another course
blank	empty
site	a place or location

TOEFL Vocabulary

transmit	to send information to a destination, often electronically
majority	the greater part of something
correspond	to communicate through written messages
via	by way of
error	an unintentional mistake

B. Learn the question type.

TOEFL Question Type

Content

What is the likely outcome of doing X then Y?

What does the man/woman imply about X?

Indicate whether each of the following was mentioned in the conversation.

• Questions asking for information to be organized into a table are more common after lectures.

• Look at your notes for relationships between the points made in the conversation.

• Pay attention to advice given and reaction to the advice for help on prediction questions.

Practice

A. Listen to the first part of the conversation and choose the correct answers.

Track 3-21

1. What is the main topic of this lecture?

   (A) The student needs help designing his website.

   (B) The student is having trouble getting his lab information off the course website.

2. How does the professor explain using the website for the class?

   (A) The professor explains that the website is used to turn in all lab assignments.

   (B) The professor explains to him the website is used to communicate and to post most lab notes.

Note-taking

B. Listen to the full conversation and take notes.   Track 3-22

Man - Student	Woman - Professor
• Having problems getting _____ _____	• Corresponds to students _____ _____
• Information is not being _____	• Asks if he has tried other _____

C. Choose the correct answers.

1. Why does the professor discuss using the wrong web address?

   (A) A blank page or error message is often the result of entering a wrong web address.

   (B) Entering the wrong web address leads to many hours on the computer trying to figure out the problem.

2. According to the student, what was the result each time the web address had been entered?

   (A) It was going straight to the page with all the lab notes.

   (B) He was getting a blank page or error message.

3. Which of the following was mentioned in the conversation?

   (A) Entering in the correct web address could be the reason nothing from the site is being transmitted.

   (B) It is a possibility the wrong web address was handed out to all the students.

TOEFL Vocabulary Practice

D. Fill in the blanks with the correct words.

transmit	majority	correspond	via	errors

1. If students rush their exams, they are more likely to make _____ on them.

2. Many business professionals travel _____ plane.

3. The radio is set up to _____ radio waves so people can listen to music.

4. A(n) _____ of votes is needed to elect a new president.

5. A professor sometimes chooses to _____ with his or her students by email.

Test

Listen to the conversation and take notes. **Track 3-23**

Woman - Student	Man - Professor
• Needs _____ • Backpack _____ _____ _____ _____ _____ _____	• Asks what the reason is • Posts all notes _____ _____ _____ _____ _____ _____

Choose the correct answers. **Track 3-24**

1. According to the student, which of the following is true?

(A) She needs the notes for the whole semester because she failed to take notes.

(B) Her computer was stolen and it had all her notes on it.

(C) If the professor didn't have the notes, she was going to drop the class.

(D) Her backpack was stolen and it had all her things in it, including her class notes.

2. What was the outcome when the student told the professor she needed all the notes?

(A) The professor told her to come back during office hours.

(B) The professor did not have notes available, so he asked her to copy one of her classmates' notes.

(C) The professor wanted to know why.

(D) The student dismissed herself to go cry.

3. Why is the student talking to the professor?

(A) She wants to know how she did on the first exam.

(B) She wants to know the web address to obtain class assignments.

(C) She wants to talk to the professor about taking a class next semester.

(D) She wants to know if she can get the class notes for the semester.

4. What is the professor's attitude toward the student?

(A) Empathetic

(B) Harsh

(C) Angry

(D) Careless

138 | Listening |

Lecture - Communication

Getting Ready to Listen

A. Learn the words.

Key Vocabulary

presentation	a type of speech, usually involving multi-media
visual aid	something used in presentations that can be seen
handout	reference material given to audience members
graph	data represented in picture form

TOEFL Vocabulary

reluctant	not eager; hesitant
comprise	to consist of
view	an opinion; belief
resolution	solution to a problem
emphasis	special significance

B. Learn the question type.

TOEFL Question Type

Content

In the lecture, the professor describes X. Indicate whether each of the following is mentioned.
Based on information in the lecture, indicate whether each sentence below describes X, Y, or Z.
Match each X with the correct classification.

- Questions asking for information to be organized into a table are more common after lectures.
- It is important to take well-organized notes while listening in order to be able to refer to them when answering organization questions.
- Be sure to order steps in a process or organize details into categories as you listen.

Practice

A. **Listen to the first part of the lecture and choose the correct answers.** `Track 3-25`

1. What is the main topic of the lecture?

    (A) How to overcome stage fright
    (B) Elements of a good presentation

2. What are the key points in this lecture?

    (A) Don't look scared, be confident, and be friendly
    (B) Be friendly, be confident, use visual aids, and use handouts

3. How does the professor describe the main topic?

    (A) By first showing an example of a bad presentation, then a good one
    (B) By discussing how each element affects the outcome of the presentation

4. Choose the best note-taking diagram for this lecture.

    (A) Concept Defining   (B) Venn Diagram   (C) Cause and Effect
        Diagram   Diagram

Note-taking

B. **Draw the diagram chosen in question 4. Then insert the information from questions 1 and 2.**

C. **Now listen to the full lecture and complete your notes.** `Track 3-26`

D. Choose the correct answers.

1. What is the likely outcome of appearing confident?

   (A) Your audience will agree with you.
   (B) Your audience will learn more from you.

2. What is the likely outcome of using visual aids?

   (A) Your audience will remember information.
   (B) Your audience will have something to review.

3. How does the professor organize the lecture?

   (A) By comparing poor speakers to good ones
   (B) By discussing the positive results of certain actions

TOEFL Vocabulary Practice

E. Fill in the blanks with the correct words.

reluctant	comprised	views	resolution	emphasis

1. An essay is _____ of an introduction, a body, and a conclusion.

2. One must come to a(n) _____ to solve a problem.

3. You should place special _____ on your work experience when writing your resume.

4. People have different _____ on controversial issues.

5. Somebody afraid of public speaking might be _____ to give a presentation in front of a class.

Test

🎧 Listen to the lecture and take notes. `Track 3-27`

Debating

- Look at issues from both sides
- Strike the hardest topic to argue
- Think about the resolution
- Anticipate arguments of other team

Debating

Cause		Effect
	→	Prepared to debate anything
	→
	→
	→

Choose the correct answers. `Track 3-28`

1. What is the lecture mainly about?

  (A) How to choose a debating topic
  (B) How to be a good debater
  (C) How debates are organized
  (D) The importance of debating skills

2. What is the likely outcome of being able to look at issues from both sides?

(A) You will be prepared to debate any topic.
(B) You will be able to choose the best topic to strike.
(C) You will be an unbiased judge in debates.
(D) You will be able to make more convincing arguments.

3. How much time do you have to prepare for the debate?

(A) 5 minutes   (B) 15 minutes
(C) 1 hour   (D) 1 week

4. What is the professor's attitude toward preparation?

(A) She thinks debaters should have more time to prepare.
(B) She thinks it is the most important part of the debate.
(C) She thinks it is hard to use one's time wisely.
(D) She thinks there should be more dialog between teams.

5. How is the lecture organized?

(A) By contrasting a good debater with a poor one
(B) By demonstrating poor debating skills through example
(C) By explaining how judges make decisions in debates
(D) By showing the results of good debating practices

6. What does the professor imply when she says this: ？

(A) The purpose is to practice debating skills.
(B) The judges won't know if you believe what you are saying.
(C) You are less likely to win if you don't agree with your teammates.
(D) The best debaters are passionate about their hobby.

Check-up

A. Choose the correct answers.

1. When answering a conversation content question
   - (A) pay attention to advice given and reaction to the advice for help on prediction questions
   - (B) pay attention to the words and phrases spoken just before and after a repeated comment to understand its context
   - (C) refer to your notes and look for repeated content words or phrases
   - (D) refer to your notes for repeated content words or phrases to give you a clue about the main idea

2. What should you do when answering a lecture content question?
   - (A) Look at your notes for any pattern to how the points are presented, such as chronologically or by importance.
   - (B) Be sure to take note of the professor's tone and any emotions expressed during the lecture.
   - (C) Look at your notes for the professor's aim for giving the lecture.
   - (D) Be sure to order steps in a process or organize details into categories as you listen.

Key Vocabulary Practice

B. Fill in the blanks with the correct words.

presentations	post	visual aids	lab
handouts	graph	blank	site

1. Teachers often use _____ to evaluate a student's oral speaking skills.

2. A _____ screen might mean that the wrong website address has been entered.

3. _____ are a good way to make sure students get all the information from a lecture.

4. In a chemistry _____, it is important to wear all the proper safety equipment.

5. Professors often use lots of _____ to keep their students' attention.

6. A construction _____ is a dangerous place to go at night.

7. Companies often use a _____ to show their yearly plans.

8. The student board is a great place to _____ announcements of upcoming concerts.

[Review 2]

🎧 Listen to the conversation and take notes. `Track 3-29`

Woman - Student	Man - Professor
• Needs some _____ • Can't find anything that can _____ _____ _____ _____ _____ _____ _____ _____	• Needs to _____ • Can start by going to _____ • Can use _____ _____ _____ _____ _____ _____ _____

Choose the correct answers. `Track 3-30`

1. What problem does the woman have?

(A) There is too much information on nature.

(B) She is having trouble finding things to defend her point of view.

(C) The professor is in a hurry.

(D) The woman's partner is not helping her.

2. According to the professor, where is a good place to find information?

(A) The government's database on nature

(B) The library

(C) In class

(D) In the professor's office

3. What does the professor imply when he says this: 🎧 ?

(A) There is too much information, so it will be very difficult.

(B) The research project will be easy.

(C) Because there is a lot of information, it will be easy.

(D) Even though there is a lot of information, it will be easy to see which parts are good.

4. What is the likely outcome of their research?

(A) They will not listen to the professor's advice, so it will be difficult.

(B) They will listen to the professor's advice, so they will do well.

(C) The will listen to the professor's advice, but still do poorly.

(D) They will choose not to do the project.

Listen to the lecture and take notes. `Track 3-31`

Communication Methods

- Telephones
- Signal Lamps
- Smoke Signals

• Call people	• Used on boats and planes	• People far away would interpret smoke patterns

Choose the correct answers. `Track 3-32`

1. What is this lecture mainly about?

(A) How people use smoke signals
(B) How people use telephones
(C) How people use signal lamps
(D) How people can communicate

2. According to the professor, who used smoke signals?

(A) Boats at sea

(B) The Chinese

(C) Airplanes

(D) Both the Chinese and Native Americans

3. Listen again to part of the lecture. Then answer the question.

How does the professor feel about the student's comment?

(A) He is angry with the student.

(B) He thinks that the student is very funny.

(C) He wants the student to be quiet.

(D) He isn't angry with the student, but he wants to keep going with the lecture.

4. What does the professor imply when he says this: ?

(A) Older communication was bad.

(B) Older communication was not as easy and it was harder to use.

(C) Today's communication is more clever than older communication.

(D) We cannot use older communication anymore.

5. How does the professor organize the lecture?

(A) He goes from best to worst forms of communication.

(B) He goes from least clever to most clever forms of communication.

(C) He discusses the most interesting form of communication first.

(D) He goes from newest to oldest forms of communication.

6. What can be inferred from the lecture?

(A) Smoke signals were very fast.

(B) Smoke signals could NOT be used in all weather and all times of day.

(C) Signal lamps were more sophisticated than telephones.

(D) Signal lamps were easy to interpret.

Listen to the lecture and take notes. **Track 3-33**

Making Laws

- The House

- The Senate

- The president

Making Laws

• Majority votes yes, bill goes to Senate	• If a majority, then goes to president	• If he or she doesn't like it, he or she can veto it

Choose the correct answers. **Track 3-34**

1. What is the main idea of the lecture?

(A) How the House is made

(B) How a law is made

(C) How a bill is made

(D) The president's options

2. According to the professor, the president has two options. What are they?

(A) He can sign the bill or veto the bill.
(B) He can contemplate the bill and sign it.
(C) He can talk about the bill and defend it.
(D) He can veto the bill and then contemplate it.

3. Listen again to part of the lecture. Then answer the question. 🎧

What does the professor imply about the bill?

(A) People are usually very friendly.
(B) People usually agree on bills.
(C) It often takes a long time for a bill to pass.
(D) People always want to make new laws.

4. What is the professor's attitude toward the process of making a bill?

(A) The House has the most important job.
(B) The Senate has the most important job.
(C) The president has the most important job.
(D) Everyone's job is equally important.

5. Why does the professor discuss the president's veto?

(A) To show the president can do whatever he wants
(B) To show that the president has a lot of power
(C) To show that Congress's actions aren't important
(D) To show how easy it is to stop a new law

6. What is the likely outcome of a bill that does not have a majority in the House?

(A) It becomes a law later.
(B) People need to contemplate it more.
(C) It will probably never become a law.
(D) The president will veto it.

Lecture 3

Listen to the lecture and take notes. `Track 3-35`

Home Remedies for

- Black eyes
- Sunburn
- Snoring
- Colds

Cause		Effect
Put cold soda can on cheek	→	
Put potato and cucumber slices on burnt area	→	
Lose weight and exercise	→	
Drink lots of orange and lemon juice	→	

Choose the correct answers. `Track 3-36`

1. What is the main idea of this lecture?

(A) How to feel better after sunburn

(B) Things you can do at home to make yourself feel better

(C) How not to get sick

(D) How to avoid going to the doctor

2. According to the professor, what is a good home remedy for sunburn?

(A) Going back into the sun

(B) Putting a cold can of soda on the burnt area

(C) Losing weight

(D) Putting slices of cucumber or potato on the burnt area

3. What does the professor imply when she says this: 🎧 ?

(A) These things don't always work for everyone but they might.

(B) These things will always make you feel better.

(C) All doctors think this will help.

(D) They're easy to do.

4. What is the professor's attitude toward home remedies?

(A) Even though they sound weird and don't always work, it's a good idea to try them.

(B) They are often very messy and sound crazy, but they can't help.

(C) Home remedies are better than going to see a doctor about pain.

(D) People should avoid getting pain so they wouldn't have to use home remedies.

5. Why does the professor discuss the problems that he does?

(A) To help us understand how we get hurt

(B) To show that injuries are common

(C) To show that home remedies can help with lots of different kinds of problems

(D) To show that home medicine can solve all our pain

6. According to the professor, which is NOT a home remedy?

(A) Exercising and losing weight

(B) Putting cucumber and potato slices on your body

(C) Drinking lots of orange juice

(D) Playing in the grass

🎧 Listen to the conversation and take notes. Track 3-37

Man - Student	Woman - Administrator
• Wants information about _____ _____ • Missing the deadline was _____ _____ • Thinking about _____ _____ _____ _____ _____ _____	• Says that deadline _____ • Can help _____ • Gives the student _____ _____ _____ _____ _____ _____ _____

Choose the correct answers. Track 3-38

1. What is this conversation mainly about?

   (A) Europe
   (C) Studying abroad
   (B) Deadlines
   (D) Studying in China

2. According to the woman, where do many students who go to Europe enjoy studying?

   (A) France
   (C) England
   (B) Spain
   (D) China

3. How does the student feel after he is told he missed the deadline?

   (A) Nervous
   (C) Disappointed
   (B) Angry
   (D) Excited

4. How is this conversation organized?
   (A) It talks about the different steps the boy must take to study abroad.
   (B) It talks about how it is the student's fault.
   (C) It talks about the advantages of studying abroad.
   (D) It is about the disadvantages of studying abroad.

Basic Skills for the
TOEFL® iBT 2

Iain Donald Binns
Micah Sedillos

Listening

Transcript & Answer Key

Transcript

[Unit 1]

Conversation

Practice

W: Hi. It looks like you are lost. Can I help you?

M: Oh, hi! Yeah I could use some assistance. This is a big campus and I am kind of lost.

W: Well, you are in luck I am a student guide!

M: Well, I have been walking around all morning looking for the student center but I can't find it.

W: Oh, it's really close. Just over there, next to the big auditorium. It is a great place to hang out and meet people. (**Practice A end.**)

M: Oh, great, I heard that, but, what is actually in there?

W: Well, the bookstore is there, so you can buy things like your books and school supplies. The school cafeteria is also a part of the student center and there are a few offices there, like the student recreation office and the student newspaper office. There is also a student lounge with a television.

M: That does sound like a great place to hang out.

W: Yeah, most students spend some time there. You can even buy tickets for concerts and plays there. Oh, and because you are a student, you will get a discount.

M: Oh, great, it sounds like there is plenty there to do.

W: There certainly is! Oh, remember to take your student ID so they can verify that you actually are a student here or they won't let you in!

M: Oh OK, thanks for you help.

Test

M: Hi, do you need any assistance?

W: Hi! Yes, is this where I buy tickets for tonight's jazz concert?

M: Yes, you can get them here, at the student center, or at the auditorium. How many tickets do you need?

W: I need to buy one for myself and one for a friend.

M: OK, can I see your student ID?

W: Here it is.

M: That's fine and is your friend a student here?

W: No, he's not. Are the tickets different prices?

M: Yes, the tickets are different prices. The non-student ticket is five dollars more than the student ticket because students that go to this university get a discount.

W: Hmm, so how much are they?

M: The student ticket is ten dollars and the non-student ticket is fifteen dollars. Do you still want them?

W: Oh, that's OK. Yeah, I'll still take the tickets.

M: Great. The total for two tickets is twenty-five dollars. We don't have the tickets here, but you can collect them at the auditorium.

W: Great, thanks. Oh, where is the auditorium?

M: It's the building next to the recreation office, and it starts at 7 p.m., so you should be there by 6:15 to collect your tickets and get a good seat.

W: Thanks so much for your help.

M: No problem. Here is your receipt. You need to show them this receipt to collect the tickets. Also, make sure to take your ID. They will want to verify the name on the tickets with your student ID.

Lecture

Practice

M: Today we're going to talk about the Egyptian Pyramids! When it comes to the pyramids, there are more questions than there are answers. But we are going to discuss examples of three things: the materials, the building, and the purpose. (**Practice A end.**)

So, what materials were these structures made of? Well, it was mainly stone. These stones were very large and heavy. They had to be moved from a quarry. Sometimes the quarry would be far away. Historians are not sure how this was done. Remember, they were built in ancient times. People didn't have the tools that we have today. So, it may have taken a huge group of slaves who were forced to pull the stones on sleds. Or, another idea is that a machine was used to roll the stones.

Then, there's how the pyramids were built. The huge stones had to be placed on top of each other. How did they lift them? We don't really know. But many people think that ramps were used. However, a whole pyramid couldn't be built with ramps alone. They wouldn't have been able to build the top. Whatever way they were built, the pharaohs who built them must have been committed! Why? Because they took many years to build!

Finally, what was the purpose? Why did they go to all this trouble? Pyramids were built for pharaohs for after they died. It was to help them move on to the afterlife. Furthermore, the pyramids would be filled with gold and things the pharaohs thought they would want and need in the afterlife.

Test

W: Who built the pyramids? Historians used to think that slaves were forced to. But it's not true. Researchers have been studying the areas around these ancient structures. They are looking at the cities that formed while they were being built.

For example, the food the builders ate shows us they were not slaves. Historians have found bakeries where bread was made to feed the workers. They have also found bones of the meat they ate. It seems that the builders ate quite well. Only the best meat for them! But, slaves are not usually fed high quality food.

Furthermore, it seems that there were different types of workers. Some were highly skilled and stayed in the cities all year. Others worked for only short lengths of time. And guess what time of year they chose? Yes, the summer! Not because it was warm, but because that is when the Nile flooded. These workers, we can guess, were farmers. They couldn't work the fields when they were flooded. So they came in to help build the pyramids for . . . maybe some money. Of course, we don't really know if they were paid. They may have been told they had to help. But that's not really the same as slavery. Or, they may have wanted to help. Maybe they felt loyal to the pharaoh. We don't really know. But, it seems that they were not forced to. Nor were they treated badly.

Another piece of evidence is graffiti. That tells us a lot about the social structure. The graffiti found does not support the idea that they were slaves. Rather, it shows groups of workers who were committed to their work.

[Unit 2]

Conversation

Practice

W: Hey, John. You are the Resident Assistant here, aren't you? Could you help me with a problem I am having with my accommodation bill?
M: Yes, Sam. What is the problem?
W: I received a housing bill and apparently I still owe money for my housing.
M: OK?
W: Well, I have already paid it. In fact, I should be due a refund because I think I paid too much! Who should I talk to? I am really concerned.
M: Are you sure you paid the bill? Did you send it to the right place?
W: Yes. I paid the bill during the student orientation.

M: OK . . . you need to go to the Office of Accommodation. They should be able to answer your questions. They may have just made a mistake. (**Practice A end.**)

W: I am positive they made a mistake. I presume they won't make me pay again!

M: No. If you have proof of payment, then you should be OK. Do you have a receipt?

W: Yes, I have a receipt.

M: Great, you should go take care of this right away so it doesn't become more of a burden than it needs to be. Once they have sorted this bill out, then they should also be able to tell you if you are due a refund.

W: You're right. I am going to go get this taken care of right now. Hopefully, the Accommodation Office is still open.

M: Its only 3 p.m., so it should be open for another hour.

Test

W: Hey, Dave. I was told you are going to be moving out of the dorm this week.

M: Yes, I am. I was going to come and talk to you. Since you're the RA, I am hoping you can answer a question for me.

W: Sure, what's your question?

M: Will I get any kind of refund from my housing payment since I am leaving early?

W: I presume you will only get a partial refund. I think you would have received a full refund if you made this decision within three weeks of orientation.

M: I guess a partial refund is better than no refund. Where do I go?

W: That is true. Apparently, you can collect refunds from the Accommodation Office, so go there first. But let me know if you have any problems.

M: Great, thanks.

W: Why are you moving?

M: Well, I don't feel like dorm life is for me; I think I made a mistake moving into the dorms. I found having three roommates a burden. I am moving in with my brother. He has moved a few blocks from the school.

W: I understand. It is hard to live with three people. One roommate is much better. You will also save money. Although, I don't know if I could live with my brother!

M: Ha ha! Well we get along really well, so I am looking forward to living with him.

W: That's good! When do you plan to move all your stuff out?

M: I should have all my stuff out by Friday.

Lecture

Practice

W: Frank Lloyd Wright changed the way houses were built in the US. He created a new architectural style. It was known as the "Prairie Style" house. He was best known for this style.

Well, what were the similarities and differences between the Prairie Styles and older styles? Well, they differed in several ways. First, the lines were different. What are the prairies like? Everything is flat, right? There are no hills. So Wright used horizontal lines a lot in his designs. These lines were dominant in his style. Prairie homes also had more open floor plans. (**Practice A end.**)

OK, so the horizontal lines made the houses blend in with the land around them. It was almost as if they were carved out of the land. Older houses, on the other hand, were like big boxes. They stood out instead of blending in. People wanted houses that looked big.

The insides of Prairie homes were different, too. Contrary to older homes, Wright's floor plans were open. Older homes had separate rooms for separate purposes. Rooms were connected to a hallway. Prairie Style homes had an open design. Rooms flowed into one another. There were fewer walls and doors. Why was this? Well, the older style suited families in past times. But families were changing. Parents were more involved with their children. They were less likely to have servants, too. So, the open design suited the new American family. That's why it was so popular. In fact, most houses built today have open floor plans.

Test

M: Today, we're going to talk about John Lloyd Wright. That's right—John, not Frank. John was Frank Lloyd Wright's son. And he, too, was an architect. He was the son of the most famous architect in the US, so what do you think he was like?

Well, for one thing, John had a good teacher—his dad! But it must have been hard, too. He was an artist. He wanted to carve a name for himself in the architectural world. He didn't want to live in his father's shadow. But he did respect his father's work. So, he wanted to learn from his father but still create his own style. If you look at his buildings, some are similar to his father's "Prairie Style." But several were quite unique.

Like his father, John made heavy use of dominant horizontal lines in his designs. But he differed from his father in how he used them. Frank Lloyd Wright used horizontal lines to make houses blend in with the flat surroundings. But John Lloyd Wright built most of his houses on hilly landscapes. The idea was still to make the house blend in with the land. They just had a different way of going about it. Furthermore, contrary to his father's use of open floor plans, John thought that separate rooms should be separated. He used solid corners and windows that were not connected to one another to achieve this effect.

John Lloyd Wright had a hard job. His father was an amazing architect. However, John had his own ideas and wasn't afraid to use them. He was able to learn from his father without copying his work.

[Unit 3]

Conversation

Practice

M: Good afternoon, Professor Johnson. I really enjoyed your lecture today. Do you have a few spare minutes to speak with me? It is about my application for the business studies graduate program.

W: Hello, William. I am glad that you enjoyed the lecture. I hope that you were paying attention.

M: Ha, ha. Yes, professor, you had my full attention.

W: I have a few minutes to spare just now. Have you completed your application yet?

M: I have a draft of it here. Would you mind having a look at it and giving me some advice on where I might improve it. (**Practice A end.**)

W: OK, let me see it. You do realize that the deadline for candidates to submit their applications is next week? This is very last minute, William.

M: Yes, professor, but I have been studying very hard all term. I will do my best in my exams.

W: Well, you will need to in order to be accepted. Now, on the first page here, perhaps you should list some of the main skills that you have picked up over the last four years here. That would be a good way to proceed after your opening statement.

M: Sure, professor, let me take a note of this.

W: Well, you have done quite a good job with this application. I have marked down a few spelling mistakes. But this looks like a good application.

M: Thank you, professor. This has really helped me a lot. Goodbye.

W: Goodbye.

Test

W: Excuse me, Professor Anderson, I'm sorry to bother you, but I was wondering if I could talk to you.

M: Yes, Mary. Have a seat. How can I help you?

W: Actually, professor, I was hoping to be of some help to you. I heard that you were looking for a student to help you with some research.

M: Ah, yes. That is correct. I need someone to help me with some of the research on the paper that I am currently working on. It is unpaid but it may help you get a better grade in class and it's good experience.

W: Um, yes, professor, that's what I have heard. I was wondering if you had picked someone to help you yet?

M: I haven't made any decisions yet. I had a lot of students apply and I am still looking at some candidates' applications. Have you submitted an application?

W: Yes, professor. And I really think I would be great for the job. I always work hard and produce good work. And, I am doing the graduate chemistry program!

M: Well, I see that you are very interested. I should tell you that the deadline for this paper is at the end of this year. So you would have to work extra hard around exam time.

W: That is fine with me, professor.

M: Well, thank you for your time, Mary. I will proceed with a few more interviews and let you know my answer soon.

W: Thank you so much, professor. Goodbye.

Lecture

Practice

M: Right, students. Today's class is on plant diseases. Last week, we talked about the different parts of a plant. Now we will learn about plant diseases. We will mainly talk about how to prevent plant diseases. Diseases are a big biological problem. That's because they are part of the ecosystem and are found in nature. They can be pretty hard to get rid of. And just like many human diseases, they are spread by germs. Germs are tiny organisms. They are too small to see. Different diseases can affect different parts of a plant. The best solution is to prevent plants from getting them. Let's talk about ways to stop diseases. **(Practice A end.)** First, you should always use clean soil. You must also water plants well. You should check plants for diseases. If you see that some plants have a disease, you must pull them out quickly.

Farmers also often grow one kind of crop, like potatoes or maize. They sell these crops as produce. Diseases spread more easily if there is a lot of one kind of plant. People will not buy produce that has been damaged. So, if farmers want to avoid losing all their crops to disease, they must keep them healthy. Planting different crops every year also prevents disease. If plants get really sick, farmers can use poison to kill the diseases. However, this is not good for the soil, the crops, or the people who eat the produce.

Test

W: Well, in class yesterday, you learned how to stop plants from getting diseases. Now it's time to look at the other major plant problem. As with diseases, this problem is also biological. It's also part of the ecosystem. Can anyone guess what it is? That's right! I'm talking about insects. There are hundreds of insects that eat plants. They make their nests and lay eggs inside plants. They also carry plant diseases. Some small insects eat just the leaves. Some large insects, like locusts, eat the whole plant! They eat leaves, fruit, stems, everything. They are very dangerous. Farmers hate locusts. In big groups, these insects can cause a lot of damage. Farmers can lose a lot of money if locusts eat their whole crop. They will not be able to sell any produce.

The way to protect garden plants and farm crops is to check plants daily. See if there are any insects or insect eggs on them and take them off. You should also pull out any dead plants and leaves you see. Insects like to hide there. If you get a new plant, keep it away from your other plants for a month or so. That way, if this plant has any insects on it, the rest of your plants won't be eaten. If plants have a lot of insects on them, some people use poison to kill them. This should only be done if there is no other plan. You see, a lot of poisons can hurt your plants, too. Even if they don't, they stay behind in the soil or air. This is not very good for the environment.

[Unit 4]

Conversation

Practice

M: Excuse me. May I speak to the manager or whoever is in charge?

W: Yes, I am the head of the canteen—Mrs. Doyle. How can I help you?

M: Ah, hello, my name is John Morrison. I am a student here at the school and I would like to talk to you about the canteen menu.

W: All right. Could you elaborate a little more?

M: Well, you see, I'd like to make a complaint. I have a wheat allergy and the food served here has wheat in it. (**Practice A end.**)

W: We do have some food with no wheat in it.

M: Sorry, I didn't mean all of the food. But there is not much that I can eat—only baked potatoes or fruit really.

W: On occasion, we serve wheat free main meals. We have a commitment to make food that everyone can eat. At the same time, we are under pressure to make food that everyone likes.

M: I understand and I would like you to serve more wheat-free food if you can. Everything seems to be made with bread or flour. I have a lot of good recipes for food without wheat that everyone can enjoy. Maybe I should give them to you; they could help to give you some inspiration.

W: That would be good. We will do our best to help you, but I can't promise anything. It is difficult to keep everyone happy.

M: OK, well thanks for your time.

W: You are welcome. Come back anytime with the recipes.

Test

W: Um, excuse me, do you work here?

M: I do, yes. What can I do for you?

W: Erm, I'm a vegan, and I was wondering what food will be served today that I can eat?

M: A vegan? That is like a vegetarian, isn't it?

W: It means that I will not eat any food that comes from an animal.

M: Oh right, so you can't eat anything from an animal? Let me see.

W: Let me elaborate, it is not an allergy. I just refuse to eat it—even dairy products like eggs, cheese, and milk.

M: I see. Well, on today's menu we have baked potatoes and, let me think.

W: Sorry to put you under pressure like this.

M: That's OK. Most of the dishes in the salad bar do not contain meat or dairy products. On occasion, they have mayonnaise in them, which is made with eggs, but not today.

W: That is great. Thank you for your help.

M: You are welcome. It must take real commitment to be a vegan. It must be difficult sometimes.

W: On occasion, there is nothing on the menu that I can eat at the canteen. I try not to make complaints because I know that it is difficult to keep everyone happy. But, it would be nice if there was more food made with vegetables and maybe rice.

M: Well, I will tell the chef. Maybe he can do more food like that.

W: That would be great. Well, today I will have the baked potato and salad. Thank you again.

M: No problem. Enjoy your lunch and have a nice day.

Lecture

Practice

W: In chemistry, we put substances into three categories. [*Slowly.*] The first is elements . . . , the second is compounds . . . , and the third is mixtures.

An element and a compound cannot be separated into different substances. But, a mixture can. Let's talk about these in more detail. (**Practice A end.**)

An element is a pure substance. It can't be separated. This is because it is made of only one type of atom. One example is oxygen. All of the atoms that make up oxygen are the same. So, you can't separate it. There are 118 elements. You can find them all on the periodic table.

OK. What is a compound? It is made from two or more elements. The atoms from these elements join together. It is difficult to separate these atoms. This makes a compound pure. An example is water. Water is made from two elements: hydrogen and oxygen. It is not easy to separate these elements. So, water is a compound.

Finally, a mixture. A mixture is also made from two or more elements. Despite this fact, it is different from a compound. How? Well, a mixture can be easily separated. This is because its atoms are not joined. So, mixtures are not pure. For example, you can add salt to water. Salt is a compound and water is a compound. But salt water is not a compound. You can easily separate the salt from the water by boiling it. The salt and the water have just been mixed together. So, it is called a mixture.

Test

M: We know of over a hundred elements. Each element is a pure substance. We can learn about elements by looking at the periodic table. Everyone who studies chemistry will learn about this table.

The periodic table is made up of rows and columns. The periodic table also has different colors. [*Slowly.*] A row is also known as a period. A column is also known as a group. And a color is also called a series.

There are seven periods and eighteen groups. Each element in a period or group has something in common. And each color is a different category of element.

When we study chemistry, the periodic table is very helpful. It tells us about their properties. It also tells us about how they behave. For example, in our periodic table all the elements that are colored blue are a type of gas. And all the elements in group one will have a big reaction when mixed with water.

Almost all the elements fit into this table but there are two rows of elements that don't fit neatly into the table. So, they are separate from the main table.

The table took a long time to make. Despite the fact that many people worked on it, Mendeleev is usually named as its inventor. Mendeleev was a Russian chemist. It was his idea to put the elements in this order. This was in 1869. It solved a lot of problems. It has been changed since then. This is because new elements have been discovered. We may have to change it again if we find more.

[Unit 5]

Conversation

Practice

M: Can I help you?
W: Oh, yeah. I need to pay a parking ticket I received a few days ago.
M: I can help you with that. Where were you parked when you received this ticket?
W: I was parked by the library.
M: OK . . . ?
W: I went into the library to check out a book. I've hurt my leg, so I can't walk to school easily and I didn't know I needed a permit to park there.
M: You need a permit to park anywhere on campus. (**Practice A end.**)
W: There was no sign to say a parking permit is needed.
M: As I said before, you need a permit to park anywhere on campus. However, this isn't a ticket; it's a warning. For your first violation, campus security gives a warning. Subsequent to a warning is a ticket.
W: Oh, good!
M: Yes, but I urge you to get a parking permit. You can park your car almost anywhere on the college campus if you have a permit.
W: Hmm . . . it would be good to be able to bring my car to school. OK, can I get a permit?
M: You can get one from the security office. All you need is your driver's license. However, if you have a note from your doctor you may be able to get a handicap-parking permit. That means you can park very close to the buildings until your leg gets better.
W: Oh, that is good! Where is the security office?
M: It's next door.
W: Thanks!

Test

W: You look lost. Can I help you?

M: Oh, yes. I need to purchase a handicap-parking permit. I received a warning from campus security and I was urged to come and get a permit.

W: I can help you with that. I need some information from you. Do you have your driver's license and license plate number with you?

M: I brought all my information with me. Here is my driver's license, my license plate number, and a note from my doctor to say why I need a handicap permit.

W: Great. It is not a hard process. It will take me a few minutes to get your information processed and get the permit ready.

M: I'm not in any hurry.

W: OK. So, you need to hang the permit in your car. A good place to hang the permit is on your rear-view mirror. If your permit can't be seen when you park in a handicap spot, you will receive a ticket.

M: Thanks for the warning. I'll make sure to leave it in my car.

W: OK, here is the permit. I just need your signature and you should be ready. Do you have any questions?

M: Actually yes, is there anywhere I can't park?

W: Well, there are signs to tell you if you can't park somewhere, so just look from them. But make sure you do check for signs. You have already received a warning, so any subsequent violations will mean getting a ticket.

M: OK. Thanks for your help today.

W: No problem.

Lecture

Practice

W: Good evening, class. Today's lecture is on patents. Last week I told you about a woman called Sheri. Sheri was the person who came up with idea of the "Jibbitz" shoe. All she did was decorate "Croc" shoes with flowers. Sheri started a retail business with her idea and made a lot of money. Now, the business world is full of rivals. There are people who want to steal good business ideas like Sheri's. They want to copy them. That is why we need to protect our ideas. The document that protects ideas is called a patent. There is a procedure you need to follow to get a patent. It can be complex, but it's worth it! There are three steps. The first thing to do when you seek a patent is to write a document. (**Practice A end.**) This document must explain what your business idea is. It should be very clearly written. It is good to ask a lawyer to help you write it. Lawyers are good at this. The second thing you do is send your document to the patent board. They will give you one year to make sure your idea is perfect. If the patent board is happy with your idea and if they are sure no one else has the same idea, they will approve it. They will give you your patent. That is the last step. Then no one else can copy your idea. The patent then lasts for twenty years. So you see, the long procedure is worth it!

Test

W: Hi, class. On Monday, we learned about the procedure to get a patent. However, that is not the only thing you should do if you are starting a business. Now, let's say you want to start making and selling something. Whatever your idea is, you should follow the same steps. Your first step should always be getting your patent. Why? Because this document stops rivals from stealing the idea. Get a lawyer to help you with this, as it can be complicated. Then, if your patent is approved, you will need money. All new businesses need money. You will need it to buy things. You will also need it to pay workers. So, where do you get it? Yes, Donald?

M: You can borrow money from a bank.

W: That's right! But remember that nothing in this world is free. The bank will ask you to pay them back over many years. They will ask you for a monthly fee. Try to pay back the money quickly. The longer it takes you, the more money it will cost you. Right, your third step is to get a place to make your product. Some people like to start small. They work from home. This is very cheap. If your business grows, however, you may need a lot more space. You may need a factory. Most big businesses use factories to make things.

Your last step is to seek good workers. I should warn you that finding good people can be difficult! They must be happy to work for you. They should be hard working. They should also be people you can trust. If you follow these steps, your business should work very well.

[Unit 6]

Conversation

Practice

W: Excuse me, Professor Chambers, are you busy?

M: Come on in. Is there something I can help you with?

W: Well, I have a question about the project that was due today. I wasn't able to turn in my final draft in class.

M: [*In a stern voice.*] Why?

W: My computer crashed last night and I lost all the work I had saved. It will be really time consuming to do it again, so is it possible to have an extension? (**Practice A end.**)

M: Well, I understand that your computer crashed and you lost all of your work. But, it is unacceptable that you waited until the last day to finish this project.

W: I know. But, I could rewrite it and have it to you by the end of next week.

M: I really can't give you a weeks extension. It is your responsibility not to wait so late to finish an important paper. It is also important to backup all your work onto a disk in case your computer crashes. Nonetheless, I will give you a couple of extra days.

W: I understand. I will try to finish it over the weekend.

M: OK, good. I will mark it on Monday. However, I am only going to give you half credit because it is late. I hope that you have learned from this.

W: I really have, professor.

M: Good luck, Rachel.

W: Thanks, Professor Chambers.

Test

W: Brian, I need to speak with you.

M: Yes, professor? Is something wrong?

W: I noticed you didn't turn in your essay in class today. Are you planning on turning it in?

M: I was going to come to your office and talk to you about an extension.

W: Why do you need an extension?

M: I can't seem to keep up with my work. I feel like I have spent all my time trying to keep up with my classes.

W: I am sorry to hear that your classes are so time consuming, but what is the reason you didn't turn in the essay today?

M: Well . . . I forgot it was due today.

W: Do you even have a draft?

M: I have it on disk but I didn't bring it.

W: Brian, this is unacceptable in college. It sounds like you need to learn how to balance your time better. Your lack of responsibility is your own fault. You need to learn to write things down.

M: But, Professor Marcy . . .

W: I'm sorry, Brian. I can't give you a full extension. Being forgetful is just not a good reason to receive an extension for any essay. Nonetheless, if you turn it in to me in the next few days I will still mark it and can give you up to half credit. However, I think you might fail this class now. Remember, you had to rewrite your last essay. So this one better be perfect!

Practice

M: We don't usually think of rocks as changing much. I mean, they might split into pieces. But other than that, they pretty much stay the same, right? Actually, this is not the case. Rocks are constantly changing from one type to another. We call this the rock cycle. The rock cycle illustrates how different types of rock are formed.

There are three main types of rocks: igneous, sedimentary, and metamorphic. Let's discuss what it is that causes these rocks to form. (**Practice A end.**)

Igneous rock is made from magma. Magma is hot, liquid rock. It is found under the Earth's surface. It is what comes out of volcanoes. When it cools, it turns into rock. Cooled magma becomes igneous rock.

Every type of rock is affected by weather. Wind and water can break rock into little pieces. They then carry them away. The pieces will land somewhere with lots of other little pieces. Over time, these little pieces of rock will stick together. When this happens, they become sedimentary rock.

Another thing that might happen to rock is that it heats up. This happens because of heat and pressure from the Earth. You see, the Earth's crust is divided into sections called plates. And these plates drift. This movement creates heat. But the rock doesn't melt. It bakes. When this happens, the rock will form crystals. It then becomes metamorphic rock. So, as you can see, rocks are always changing via the rock cycle.

Test

W: Continental drift is when the plates on the surface of the Earth move. This is constantly happening and it explains a lot about the Earth. As the plates move around, they cause certain events. Of course, the plates drift very slowly. So, it takes many years to see the effects of their movement.

When plates crash together, they create mountains, volcanoes, and earthquakes. As all of these things happen, a lot of rock gets broken up. The bits of rock are buried in the hot Earth. Then they heat up. They may even melt and rise back up again. Then the melted rock might return to the surface through a volcano.

At the same time, plates move away from other plates. This creates a rift. Something has to fill in the space left behind. The thing that does this is hot magma. It comes up from beneath the Earth and forms volcanoes. Again, earthquakes occur as a result of the movement of the plates.

The other thing that happens is that plates slide past each other. For example, we might have two plates side by side. One might move south while the other moves north. No mountains or volcanoes are formed from this movement. But it can cause a lot of earthquakes.

The land around us illustrates the history of continental drift. When we see a mountain range, we know that two plates have been crashing into each other for some time. When we see a large rift, we know the plates are moving apart. When an area has a lot of earthquakes, we know that it is on the edge of a plate. That plate might be sliding past another one. It is an endless cycle that is slowly changing our planet.

[Review 1]

Conversation 1

[*Knock on door.*]
M: Come in!
W: Hi, Dr. Stevens.
M: Hi, Tara. What can I help you with today?
W: Well, I'm applying to grad school and . . .

M: Good for you. Have you taken the GRE?

W: Yes, I think I did well.

M: Good. I think you would be an excellent candidate for graduate studies.

W: Thanks, I'm glad to hear you say that. I was going to ask if you wouldn't mind writing me a letter of recommendation.

M: I'd be more than happy to. Let me see, when do you need to submit your application?

W: Well, it's due February 1st.

M: OK, I can have it ready by Friday. Now, can I give you any further assistance with the application procedure?

W: I appreciate it, but I think I've got it under control.

M: OK, well let me know if there is anything I can do to help. I know you seniors are under a lot of pressure. You're working on your thesis, trying to keep up with your course work, and on top of that you're applying to grad school.

W: Yeah, it's hard to stay on top of things. But I'm managing. I still need to write the essays for my application, though.

M: Well, you've still got plenty of time. As I said, I'll have your letter ready Friday. Let me know which schools you are applying to and I'll send it along. Have you arranged to have your transcripts sent?

W: Yes, I have. Thank you so much, Dr. Stevens.

M: No problem. Good luck with your application.

Lecture 1

W: These days, people are concerned about the planet. We don't want to pollute the air. We don't want to waste water. Some people think about these things in their architectural designs. They are committed to the Earth. They don't want the structures they build to be a burden. The concept is called "Green Architecture."

There are three main things to think about. One is energy. The second is orientation. And the third is materials. Let's look at energy. The home will have to be heated when it's cold. And it will have to be cooled when it's hot. What's the best way to do this? By keeping energy loss low. So you need to insulate the building. That way warm air or cold air stays inside.

The orientation of the building is important. If the structure is placed just right, it will get more energy from the Sun. That's clean energy. Large windows are used in the walls facing south. This is so the heat can get in. North facing walls will have few windows. This is so the heat can't get out.

Finally, the materials used are important. Some materials are good for hot climates. They hold out heat during the day. That's when you don't want the house to be hot. Then, at night when it cools off, the heat gets into the house. That saves energy. Materials can be chosen for other reasons. Some use recycled materials. That is less wasteful. Some use wood from trees that were replanted.

Lecture 2

M: We're going to talk about owning a business. To form a business, you need to get a business license. You also need to decide what type of business it will be. How do you decide? OK, there are two main options. Well, presuming you are the only owner. Let's look at them. One is sole proprietorship. The other is incorporation.

Those are big words. Allow me to elaborate. Sole proprietorship just means that you are the only owner. But you can be the only owner of a corporation. So, what's the difference? First, there's debt. If the company goes in to debt, so do you. The company might fail. But you will still have to pay back the money. Then, there are taxes. The owner pays taxes—the business doesn't. The owner earns money from the company. He or she pays taxes on that.

Is this unacceptable? Do you prefer more security? You can form a corporation. You are still the owner. You have control. But, the company is separate from you. The company can take out a line of credit. You are not responsible for it. The company has to pay it back. Say the company fails. You won't have to pay that money back. Taxes are another matter. The company pays taxes. And the owner pays taxes. The owner is taxed on income from the company.

So, there are pros and cons to both. It's up to you to decide what works best for you.

Lecture 3

W: How do we get energy? How do we get water? How do we get nutrients? Through our mouths, right? But what about plants? They don't have mouths. Even if they did, they couldn't move around to find food. How do they survive? Today, we're going to look at how plants are able to live. Not only that, but how plants make more plants?

So, let's look at the first problem. Energy. Plants need energy to grow. Where do they get it? They get it from the Sun. That's why plants need sunlight—to grow! They turn the energy from the light into sugars. That way they can store the energy. And they can use it to grow. This is an important biological function and it's called photosynthesis.

What about water? All organisms need water to live. Plants too. Where do they get it? From rain, of course. But not through their leaves. They take rain from the soil. They do this using their roots. Through their roots, they take in water from the soil. Furthermore, plants need nutrients. And they get it the same way they get water. There are nutrients in the soil. Plants take them in through their roots.

Plants are very important to an ecosystem. Many animals rely on plants for food. So, it is important that species of plants continue. In other words, they need to reproduce. But how do plants make more plants? Well, there are several ways. But we're going to talk about pollination. Some plants create pollen. Then this pollen gets carried away. Maybe by a bee. Or maybe by the wind or water. But if it lands on another plant just like it, it will create a new plant. That's how flowers reproduce and continue to contribute to the ecosystem.

Conversation 2

M: Excuse me. Is this the Student Center?
W: It sure is. How can I be of assistance?
M: Well, I'm seeking employment. Are there any jobs available?
W: Oh, you're a bit late in applying for work. Usually people apply in the spring for jobs starting in the fall.
M: I know. I didn't know I was going to need a job. See, I have a scholarship to pay for my studies. But apparently it doesn't cover my accommodation. I tried to get a student loan to pay for my housing. Unfortunately, my application wasn't approved.
W: Oh dear. I understand. Well let me see if we have anything. Sometimes students drop out early in the fall semester and their jobs become available. Let's see . . . a-ha! How about security?
M: Well . . . I don't really have any experience. Is there much training?
W: Sure, you'll work with a senior security guard. He or she will help you learn the ropes.
M: OK, well, that sounds great, then. How do I proceed?
W: Here's an application form. Just fill it out and drop it off here. We'll give you a call to work out the details. You'll probably get a call by the end of the week. Then, you can collect your uniform at the security office.
M: Fantastic. Is there much competition?
W: You'll be the first person to apply. I don't know if the position is being advertised, so you might get lucky.
M: Great, well, thank you very much for all of your help.
W: You're welcome. Good luck!

[Unit 7]

Conversation

Practice

W: Excuse me. I am looking for someone who can help me. I need to pay for my classes.

M: I can help you.

W: I received this bill in the mail. (**Practice A end.**)

M: OK. Did you already register for the courses you want to take this semester?

W: There is one course I still might consider. Would you be able to tell me if there is open enrollment for the class?

M: Yes. What class is it?

W: Art history.

M: Let me see. I apologize for this taking so long, my computer is slow . . . OK, here it is. It looks like the class does have open enrollment. Would you like to register for it?

W: I would. I was enrolled for it last semester but the class was canceled because not enough students signed up. So, I had to switch classes.

M: Well, hopefully that won't be the case this semester. I have you enrolled as a full-time student with five classes. Does that sound right?

W: Yes.

M: All I need from you now is at least half the tuition. The other half is due by the first day of class.

W: OK. Do I mail the other half of my tuition to you?

M: It would be best if you paid in person at the administration office.

W: What if I decide to drop a class after I pay?

M: You will receive a refund if you drop the class within the first two weeks. After two weeks, you are not guaranteed a refund.

W: Thanks for your help.

M: No problem.

Test

W: I understand you want to drop your art history class, John. What is the reason?

M: It's not what I had expected. I want to drop the class while I can still receive a refund.

W: It is two days past the drop date. You are only going to receive a partial refund.

M: Are you sure? Someone at the administration office told me I had until today to drop a class and receive a full refund.

W: Do your remember who you spoke to?

M: Yes, his name is Derrick.

W: OK, I will give him a call.

M: Thanks.

W: I apologize, John. You do have until today to drop a class. I would recommend you consider registering for a less time-consuming class like weight training. That way you could still be enrolled as a full-time student. The weight training class has open enrollment so you should not have a problem getting into the class two weeks into the semester.

M: I do want to remain a full-time student. Could you enroll me in weight training?

W: I will do that right now. You do understand you will not be receiving a refund now because you are switching classes.

M: Yeah, I understand. I want to be enrolled as a full-time student. Thanks for your help, Ms. Foster.

W: Let me know if you have any more problems with your schedule.

Lecture

Practice

M: Hello class. Last week we studied a book by the writer, Jane Austen. Some of you have requested that I tell you more about her. So, in today's class, we will have a very general look at her life. I expect that a few of you know a little about her already but if you want to know even more, you could read her biography. Now, let's learn a little about her early life, middle life, and later life. (**Practice A end.**)

Austen was born in England in 1775. She was part of a very big family. She had six siblings. She revealed her writing talent at a young age. She began her first novel when she was just fourteen years old.

When she was older, Austen fell in love with a young man called Thomas Lefroy. They never married. No one is sure why. Many people think that Lefroy inspired the character, Darcy, from her book, *Pride and Prejudice*. She started to write this novel around the time she met him. It took her two years to write it. Her first novel was published in 1811.

In her later life, Austen moved to a town called Bath. By then she was famous. Many people loved her books. They thought she was a sophisticated writer. They also thought she was intelligent and they liked her humor. In 1816, Austen began to get very sick. She died one year later, in 1817. She was only forty-two years old. Her death was a big loss.

Test

W: OK. Let's look at three women writers who all wrote famous books after Jane Austen. We don't have much time, so I will just give you some general information. I expect some of you would like to know more, so I have their biographies here. You may borrow these from me after class. I have also requested that the library get a few copies. Anyway, the three writers are Emily Bronte, George Eliot, and Virginia Woolf.

Emily Bronte was born in 1818, one year after Jane Austen died. She published one book called *Wuthering Heights* in 1847. She first published it under a man's name, Ellis Bell. Three years later, she published the same book under her own name. Emily died in 1848 when she was only thirty. Her siblings, Charlotte and Anne, also wrote novels. Many people feel that Emily's work was more sophisticated than her sisters' were but I am not so sure.

George Eliot's real name was Mary Anne Evans. She was born in 1819. Like Emily Bronte, she also published novels under a man's name. At this time, many people did not think women were intelligent enough to be good writers. Evans's most famous book is called *Middlemarch*. It revealed a lot about life in a small town in England. It was published in 1872. Evans died in 1880 having lived a long and happy life.

Our third writer is Virginia Woolf who was born in 1882. Woolf liked George Eliot's novels. She also wrote a lot about the First World War. Her books are very sad because she had a sad life. Her most famous book is called *To the Lighthouse*, published in 1927. Woolf died in 1941. She killed herself. There were many reasons for this. One was that she was sad about the Second World War.

[Unit 8]

Conversation

Practice

M: Good afternoon. My name is Michael Morris. I was wondering if you could help me. I am about to finish my first year of a history degree and I am considering studying abroad for a semester. Could you tell me what my options are?

W: Certainly, Mr. Morris. Let me look at your details on the computer. May I have your student ID card please?

M: Yeah, sure. Here you are.

W: Thank you. Now let me see. You are taking a history degree you say. Well we have a few options for studying abroad for a semester in your second year. We have partnerships and exchange programs with schools in different parts of the world. Is there anywhere that you would like to study in particular? (**Practice A end.**)

M: Actually, yes, I would really like to study in France.

W: Well, we do have an exchange program with a school in Paris that you may be interested in. You could study world history there for a semester next year.

M: That sounds great. I have some family in France, so that would be perfect for me.

W: Can you speak French at all?

M: A little bit, yes.

W: Good, that won't be an issue then. Knowing the language will help you settle in. Now, if you would like, I can send you the details about the school, the course, and any immigration issues?

M: That would be great. Thank you very much.

W: No problem, Mr. Morris. I will gather the information and forward it to you tomorrow. Goodbye.

Test

W: Hello, my name is Elena Garcia. I am a student from Mexico. I arrived last semester and am having a few problems. Can someone here help me?

M: Hello, Ms. Garcia. Well, this office is here to help students from abroad with any issues that they may have, so I think I can help! Are you here as an exchange student?

W: Yes, I am, this university and mine have a partnership, and I will be here for a year. I am struggling a little with the language; my English is still not so good so I am finding some of the classes and essays difficult.

M: Oh, I see. Don't worry. You have a couple of options. You can change your classes to easier ones or we can provide you with a student tutor to help you.

W: Wow, thank you so much. This is such good news for me. I think a tutor would be best. Actually, I also got a letter saying I need to fill out a form for immigration, but I don't know where to get it. Maybe you can tell me that as well?

M: No problem. I can forward the forms you need. They are quite simple but if you need help with them come and see me.

W: Thanks so much. I am sure that this will help me to settle in more easily.

M: That's good. If you write down your details here, we will arrange a tutor for you and I will forward the forms.

Lecture

Practice

M: Today, I want to compare how people and communities can help the environment. We can do many things. (**Practice A end.**)

Helping the environment can start with one person. There are many easy ways to help. You can adjust the amount of water, electricity, and gas that you use. A small change can have a big impact. You can also help by initiating projects. One person or a whole community can start a project! Things such as picking up trash can help. You can do that on your own. Or even get all the schools in your community to help! Projects like this can make people aware of their impact on the environment.

Recycling is also very easy. Having places in the community to take paper, or glass, is great. But if you don't have that then you can also reuse paper and bottles. Or even just try to make less garbage.

For very big changes to happen, each community and country around the globe needs to help. They can legislate how much people pay for gas, water, and electricity. They can make a tax for people who use too much. This is a fair way to make people use less. They can also pass other laws. These laws can punish people who hurt the environment.

Any one person can make changes. But, if we are all strict, and the community makes laws to help the environment, then great changes can be made.

Test

W: Professor, I don't understand. How do communities work together to make big changes?

M: That's an excellent question. What is the biggest community you can think of?

W: Uh, maybe a city?

M: Yes, but think bigger.

W: Ah, a country!

M: Excellent—a country! This leads me to our next topic. We will study how people around the globe help the environment. Today, we will look at two countries and how they help the environment: the US and the UK.

The best way that the UK and the US help is to legislate against things that are bad for the environment. Both have taxes to help people lower their impact on the environment. But in the US they have low taxes and in the UK very high taxes. Anyone buying gas in both these countries will quickly be aware of the difference. Gas in the UK is much more expensive than in the US. Sometimes it is two or three times more. People might think this isn't fair. However, because of this people in the UK use more public transport and often buy smaller cars than people in the US. This is better for the environment.

The UK and the US also work to limit smoke in the air. The UK has legislated how much smoke a factory can make. They punished people who hurt the environment badly. These people had to pay a lot of money. So, factories had to adjust how much smoke they produced. In the past, though, the US hasn't had strict laws. But now, they too are passing strict laws on how much smoke can be put in the air.

[Unit 9]

Conversation

Practice

M: Excuse me, Professor Murphy. May I have a word with you?
W: Hello, James! Yes, I have a few minutes to spare. What would you like to talk about?
M: Great. I was hoping for a little advice from you actually. I have been invited to enter an essay competition for students. However, I am not sure what to write about. (**Practice A end.**)
W: I see, James. First of all, congratulations on being invited to enter the competition. I know that was an ambition of yours, and a number of teachers have been praising your writing for a while. What type of essay are you expected to write?
M: Well, it is to be about something that I like and my interpretation of it. Perhaps a review of a book I like, or something about my favorite painting. I am having trouble choosing one thing to write about. There are so many options.
W: I am glad that you are really contemplating this. In the past, you have written some good essays on books. Maybe you should write about one of your favorite books.
M: Yes, I was thinking that might be the best option. However, I'm worried that I might not do a good job.
W: Give lots of reasons and examples. Remember you want to convince the people who read your essay that you have really thought about the book.
M: That's true. Thank you, professor. You've helped me a lot.
W: You're welcome, James. Good luck.

Test

W: Hi, Professor Jones. How are you?
M: I am very well thank you, Ashley. How are things with you?
W: I am OK thanks.
M: I heard that you were asked to show your artwork at the university art show. Congratulations! You must be very excited.
W: Well, yes, it is great. It has been an ambition of mine. But, to be honest, I am nervous about it.
M: Oh, I see. Will this be your first show?
W: Yeah.
M: You shouldn't worry. I have seen your art and I am convinced everyone will love it.
W: Thanks, professor. I have had a lot of praise from my teachers, which is really nice. But I have been contemplating the reaction to my work from others.

M: Ah, I understand what you are saying. That will be a new experience for you.

W: Yes, a number of teachers and professionals will review my art and discuss their interpretation of it with me. That really worries me.

M: You have to remember that everybody's opinion and interpretation of art is different.

W: I know—that's what scares me!

M: Well, as an artist, you must remember that you cannot control what people see in your work. You just have to do your best.

W: I guess that you are right. I will enjoy the good reviews and forget the bad ones! Thanks for the advice.

M: No problem, Ashley. Good luck with the show.

W: Thanks. Have a nice day, professor.

Lecture

Practice

M: How many of you want to be able to study better? People often have many problems studying. Problems such as finding it hard to concentrate, feeling lazy and unhealthy, and finding it difficult to start studying. These are all related to your brain. You can make a few small changes, such as changing your diet, sleeping patterns, and doing more exercise, to help solve these problems. And they all help your brain and so help you study. (**Practice A end.**)

How many people here find it hard to concentrate on their work? Well this could be a symptom of tiredness. Sleep helps your brain work better. Your body needs a minimal amount of sleep every night. Not enough or too much sleep equates to a body and brain that doesn't work as well as it can.

How many of you feel lazy and unhealthy? This feeling can make it hard to study. Your brain has so many things that it must do. You can help your brain by eating healthy food. Implementation of a new diet can help you study better. Healthy foods with a high-energy output help your brain have more energy. On the other hand, foods with lots of sugar and fat can make your body and brain feel lazy. Try to exclude foods with high sugar content. But if you can't, only eat small quantities.

Finally, how many of you find it difficult to start your work? This is because you have too much energy. Go to the gym and exercise. When you go home, you will feel better and more alert. So, you will also be able to sit and study better.

Test

W: OK. So, many people believe in having a balanced lifestyle. This is when people make sure to do many different things. You don't concentrate all your energy on one thing. This can make you feel bad. You should use your energy for lots of things.

M: Professor? Are you telling us to relax more and to not always study?

W: Ha ha! That is exactly what I am saying!

M: My friend never studies! But he plays computer games in his room all day. I think it is boring and I don't want to be his friend anymore.

W₂: Well, my brother is a really good student. But he doesn't do anything but study. And, he is always sick.

W: Well, neither of them have balanced lifestyles. You shouldn't spend all your time doing just one thing whether it be studying or playing on the computer.

Tell your friend that he needs to spend time with his friends or he might lose them. Too much time by yourself can equate to a loss of friends. It is important to make enough time for both.

And tell your brother to go to the gym and spend some time having fun. And most importantly, tell him to sleep more. These things will make him happier, healthier, more alert, and even help him concentrate on his studies. Implementation of a balanced lifestyle can help both of them.

In fact, even big companies around the world are telling their workers to get balanced lifestyles. These companies saw that workers who only spent a minimal amount of time with their families were not happy. However, people who had a good balance were often happy. Their output at work was better. So, the companies started to tell all the workers about having a good balance.

[Unit 10]

Conversation

Practice

W: Good morning. What can I do for you?
M: Hello there, I was wondering if you could help me? I have lost my student identification card. I am not sure what I should do now.
W: I see. May I have your name and student ID number so that I can look up your details on the student database? (Practice A end.)
M: I'm sorry I can't remember my student number. I am a new undergraduate here and it was written on my ID card. My name is Andrew Mills and I am studying in the English program in my first year.
W: All right. Let me see if I can find your details.
M: I am sorry for the trouble.
W: That is all right, lots of students lose their ID cards. Ah, here are your details. So you would like to declare your card stolen?
M: I don't think that it was stolen; I just misplaced it.
W: I see. Your details indicate that you also lost an ID card just over a month ago.
M: Yes, that is correct. I've not had a lot of luck with my student cards.
W: You should be more careful in the future. Losing your card anytime is quite serious but losing two cards in one term is very careless. You will have to pay a fee for the replacement one this time.
M: Oh, right. I'm sorry, it won't happen again.
W: All right, here is your new card. Take care of this one Mr. Mills.
M: Thank you, I will.

Test

W: Hello, my name is Jane Simpson. I am a third year undergraduate nursing student and I would like a replacement student ID card please.
M: I see. Good morning, Jane. May I ask why you need a new student card? Have you misplaced your old one?
W: No, I actually still have my old student card here. It is just that it is very old now. I got it when I first started studying here over two years ago, so I would like a new one.
M: Do you realize that you must declare your student card lost, damaged, or stolen in order to be able to be issued with a new one? Is there anything wrong with your current ID card? Can I see it?
W: Here you go.
M: I see nothing wrong with it. It looks perfectly fine to me.
W: Well, it is just that my picture looks very old and I really don't like it anymore. I look different now from when I was in my first term on campus. Really, I would just like a new photograph on my card. Is that possible? I would really appreciate any help that you could give me.
M: I am sorry, Jane, but once your photo is in our database we can't update it. Otherwise, we would need to give out new ID cards to students anytime they change their hair or style. There is nothing I can do for you.
W: Oh, right. Well thank you for your time anyway. Goodbye.

Practice

M: OK. So, Sony is one of the biggest names in Japan. It makes electronics such as TVs, MP3 players, and so on. You may own a Sony product yourself. My electronics are predominantly Sony. Today, I'm going to tell you the three secrets to Sony's success. One is innovation. Another is listening to the consumer. And the third is self-reliance. (**Practice A end.**)

Sony is always trying to improve its products. Their products have gone through many phases to make them more durable. And to make them more advanced. You have to stay competitive. Other firms are trying to make a better product than yours. So you have to stay ahead. You have to put the money and time into it. Sony's name is known for quality. They were the first to come out with portable radios. And they kept improving them.

It's very important to listen to people. These people might buy your product. Years ago, Sony came out with a tape recorder. An opera student told them it wasn't very good. And they listened. She told them why it wasn't good. She told them how they could improve it. So they did. They made a better tape recorder.

Finally, they became self-reliant. They did not want to commission other firms to make materials for them. So, they started making their own. They started making their own plastics and stuff. This saves on costs. The savings allow them to put more into innovation. And that's why Sony thrives today.

Test

W: The best cars in the world are predominantly Japanese. In fact, the Japanese car industry is the largest in the world. But how did it get to be so big? We're going to look at the history of car making in Japan. It can be divided into three major phases: pre-war, World War II, and post-war.

In 1923, there was an earthquake. There was a lot of damage. People needed to get around. Trucks were brought from the US to help. American firms then realized that they could make a lot of money in Japan. So they set up a company in Japan. Until the war, most cars in Japan came from abroad. Still, there were a few local car makers.

The second phase was "World War II." This includes the years leading up to it. Since their last war, the Japanese military saw the need for cars and trucks. They commissioned firms to make them. The government made rules that made it hard for American firms to stay competitive. So, the American firms left. Then came World War II. The government had a lot of control. Car makers couldn't work on cars for people. They were all for the military. The government control meant that car makers were not competitive. They worked together. This helped to improve the technology a lot.

After the war, the government stopped controlling the industry. Car makers were free to do what they wanted. But the government encouraged them to get better. The industry then thrived. They developed the most durable cars in the world.

[Unit 11]

Conversation

Practice

M: Excuse me. Is this the IT center?
W: Yes. What can I do for you?
M: I am having a bit of trouble with my laptop computer. I think that it might have a virus or something.
W: I see. Do you have it with you? I could have a quick look at it now if you would like.
M: That would be excellent, thanks. Here you are. I have a lot of assignments due and there is information on my computer that I need to finish them. I don't know what I'll do if I've lost all of my files. (**Practice A end.**)

W: I understand. I'll do my best to help you. What exactly is wrong with it?

M: When I turn it on, the screen just freezes and I can't open any files.

W: All right. Do you have an anti-virus program on your computer?

M: I am not sure. What is that?

W: It is a program on your computer. It defends it from any viruses that may attack it. It is very important to have this on your computer.

M: I see. I am not sure, but it is normally quite resistant to viruses. I have never had this problem before.

W: OK, well I see here that you do have a virus. I will install another anti-virus program and you should be able to carry on normally with your tasks in a few hours. Could you come to pick up your computer at 3 p.m.?

M: Yes, no problem. Thank you so much!

Test

W: Hello. My laptop computer has stopped working. I was hoping that you could have a look at it for me?

M: Sure. Can I see your student card, please?

W: Yes, here you are. I dropped it and now it won't turn on and I have a big assignment to finish.

M: Oh dear, that's not good. Laptop computers are not too resistant to being dropped, I am afraid. May I see it?

W: Yes, here it is. It looks OK; it's not cracked or anything. It was in my bag when I dropped it.

M: That is good. A padded laptop bag is a good way to defend your computer from things like this.

W: I see. I hope that saved it. I have a lot of important files on it.

M: Well, you can see here that when I plug in the computer, the light on the battery comes on. This hopefully means that the computer itself is all right. The power button was probably broken in the fall. That is why you cannot turn it on.

W: OK, can you fix it?

M: Normally we don't do this kind of repair. The IT center is really for support only. However, it is quiet here today and fixing a power button is not a big task, so I will see what I can do for you.

W: Oh, thank you so much! That is very kind of you!

M: You're welcome. Can you come back later?

W: Sure, see you later.

Lecture

Practice

M: OK. Who wants to become president of the United States? In today's class, we are going to talk about how to do that! It is a long process. But one that is straightforward.

America has two different political parties. They have different ideas. They also think different things are important. But they are both very strong. Most candidates for president come from the two parties.

First, they must declare that they want to be president. They must also choose which party they will be in. After this, there is an election within each party. Each state decides which person is the best in their party. (**Practice A end.**) Candidates talk to lots of people. They try to distinguish themselves. This takes a long time. It also costs a significant amount of money.

Next, all the people from the parties convene in a city. The winner is announced. This person will then be in a bigger election.

The big election is when the people choose the president. They decide who they like. Candidates go around the country talking to people. They tell people about their ideas. They hope people like them. They make legitimate efforts to make everyone happy. This takes even more time. It costs even more money as well. On Election Day, Americans choose who will be the next president. The candidate who gets the most votes is the winner. He or she is the new president. He or she will be president for the next four years, unless they are impeached.

Test

W: Professor. What happens if the people don't like the president? Can they choose a new one?

M: Unfortunately, they cannot do that. They have to wait four years for another election.

W: What if the president does something really bad?

M: That is an excellent question. If the president does something that is against the law, he can be impeached. This is a trial. Congress decides if the president can still be president.

W: How does this work?

M: The process is pretty straightforward. First, the Congress needs to know what happened. Many things are said about the president. So they need to know if it is legitimate. Congress will convene if it is a big problem. The lower house of Congress decides if the president did something significant to break the law. If so, then they impeach the president. This means that he has to be on trial. It is just like in court. The upper house then does their job. They have to ask questions during the trial. They need to learn exactly what happened. They then decide if the president should stay. All the members of the upper house must vote. Over sixty-seven percent of the upper house needs to think the president did something wrong. Over sixty-seven percent means that the president must quit.

W: Is there another election after this?

M: No, the vice president then becomes president.

W: Has any president ever quit?

M: Yes, Richard Nixon quit on August 9, 1974. He did this during the trial. Presidents Bill Clinton and Andrew Johnson also had trials. But the upper house didn't think that they did anything wrong.

[Unit 12]

Conversation

Practice

M: Professor Davis, I was wondering if you could help me?
W: Sure, what are you having trouble with, Fred?
M: I have been having problems getting the information you posted online for today's lab. It gives an error message saying that the information can't be transmitted.
W: Hmm . . . OK, we need to fix that. The majority of lab notes go online and I ask all the students to correspond with me, and each other, via the website. Can you explain exactly what is happening? (**Practice A end.**)
M: Well, when I go to the website I get the error message or the page is just blank.
W: Have you tried going to other sites?
M: Yes, I get on other sites fine
W: And have you tried using another computer?
M: Yes, but I always get the same error message or blank page.
W: It sounds like you don't have the correct web address. Entering in the wrong web address could be the reason nothing from the site is being transmitted. I will write it down for you. After we speak, I want you to go and see if it works.
M: Thank you, Professor Davis.
W: Not a problem. I'm glad you came and got this taken care of quickly. I may have given the wrong web address to all the students. I will put a notice up to say what the correct site is. But, please let me know if it doesn't work.
M: OK, professor.

Test

M: Hi Lauren. What can I do you for you?

W: Professor Thompson, is it possible to get some lecture and lab notes from you?

M: From this week's lecture?

W: Actually, I need all the lecture and lab notes since the start of the semester.

M: That is a lot of notes. Why do you need so much?

W: Yesterday I set my backpack down while I went to the restroom and it was stolen. It had all my notes in it for the majority of my classes.

M: Oh no! What a nightmare! Did you have any money in it?

W: I had everything: money, credit cards, notes, books . . . . It's so annoying.

M: Well, I will make getting the notes for this class easy then. I teach classes online and I correspond with those students via the website. So, I post all my notes there. I will give you access to the site for a few days and you can print the notes from there.

W: That would be great. It will save me a lot of time from copying someone's notes.

M: Yeah, oh but sometimes the site has trouble transmitting the videos and pictures I post. It sometimes just shows a blank page or an error message, but if you just type in the web address again you will see them.

W: That's good to know.

M: Anything else?

W: That's it. Thank you so much for your help.

M: Not a problem. Let me know if it works.

Lecture

Practice

M: Most people are reluctant to give presentations. It can be scary. But there are a few tools you can use to make it easier. For one thing, don't just stand up and talk. We will look at three things you can do to improve your presentation. A good presentation is comprised of being friendly, being confident, using visual aids, and giving handouts. The effect of these elements will be an audience that listens, learns, and understands your view on the issue. (**Practice A end.**)

Of course, the speaker is important. You should look open and friendly. This will make your audience trust you. And you should look confident. Then your audience will be more likely to agree with you. Perhaps you are debating or proposing a resolution. If so, show that you believe what you are saying. Your audience will be more likely to believe it, too.

Using visual aids is also helpful. First, they can help you make a point. Use a simple graph to show a trend. That will stick with your audience. It's better than simply telling them about a trend. Secondly, visual aids can help to put emphasis on key points. Put your key points on a screen. It helps your audience follow along.

Lastly, it is a good idea to give out handouts. This gives your audience something to take with them. If they want to remember a fact, they can look it up. This way they are more likely to learn something from you. They have something to review.

Test

W: A debate is a formal argument. One team agrees with a statement. The other disagrees. They each try to convince judges that they are right. We're going to discuss things you can do to help you win a debate.

To be a good debater, you need to be able to argue both sides of an issue. It doesn't matter what your view really is. So you should get used to looking at issues from both sides. Then you'll be prepared if you have to debate. In debates, you pick your side before you know the topic. You choose to be "for" or "against" before you know what the issue is.

There may be issues you are reluctant to argue. That's why you are given some choice. Three statements are issued. Each team can strike one statement. So, you should think about how hard it will be to argue your side of a topic. Then you can strike the hardest topic. That way you don't have to argue something you disagree with.

You have fifteen minutes to prepare. You must use your time wisely. First, think about the resolution. The "for" team presents it. The "against" team argues against it. So you should think about what the resolution will mean. If you were "for," why would it be good? If you were "against," why would it be bad?

Then you must think of the other team's arguments. You have to guess what they are going to say. Then you have to say why they are wrong. If you know what they are going to say, you will be ready. Place special emphasis on your strong points. A debate is comprised of arguments. The team with the best arguments wins. So have an argument for every point the other team makes.

[Review 2]

Conversation 1

W: Hi, professor. Do you have a few minutes?

M: Uh, well, I need to go to class, so make it quick.

W: Ah, OK, it's pretty straightforward. I was wondering if you could give me some advice.

M: Sure, go ahead.

W: I am having problems with our group assignments. I can't find anything that can defend our point of view.

M: What is your point of view?

W: We are saying that it is good for the globe to protect nature. I want to convince everyone that we are right.

M: Ha, I didn't know that you were so competitive. I would start by going to the library and asking for some help there.

W: OK, I did that, but I didn't find anything so great.

M: Hmmm . . . . Well, how about using the database from the government's commission on nature?

W: I hadn't thought of that.

M: There is a significant amount of information. More importantly, there is a lot of information that will help you to defend your position. There is a lot of information there, so it will take a long time to go through it all. The good parts will distinguish themselves easily.

W: Wow! Thanks, professor. I'll get my group together and we will go start our research tonight.

M: No problem. I've got to run. I don't want to be late. See you in class!

W: Bye.

Lecture 1

M: OK class. Today, we are going to talk about communication. We will start with an easy question. How do you talk to someone far away?

M2: You yell. [*Everyone starts giggling.*]

M: Ha ha, very funny. [*Playfully.*] But seriously . . . how do you talk to people far away?

W: I pick up my phone. I call them.

M: Excellent answer! You pick up your phone. You call. Today's communication is very easy and sophisticated. In the past, long distance communication was terribly difficult. It was important to talk during things like war. It was so important that people made some great innovations. So, they learned how to communicate without telephones.

The signal lamp is a way people talked without phones. These used to be everywhere. These used very strong lamps. People put a shade in front of the lamp. This blocked the light. The patterns of light meant different things. This let people transmit messages via sight. Each person had a task. One person had to send the signals. The person who saw it also had an assignment. He had to write down the message. This was often used on boats at sea. It was also used to help airplanes.

Native Americans and the Chinese used smoke signals. These transmitted important messages during battle. They put a blanket over a fire. They would then quickly remove the blanket. This would make a cloud of smoke. People far away could see the clouds. They would then interpret these clouds. Then they told their people what to do.

Lecture 2

M: Today, I am going to teach you how America legislates. So, first of all, does anyone know the two most important parts of the law making process?

W: Yeah, it's the president and the Congress.

M: Very well done! The president and the Congress. Congress is comprised of two parts. The lower house is called the House of Representatives. It's often called the "House" for short. The upper house is called the Senate. Everyone must work together.

To initiate a new law, a person in the Congress needs to write a new bill. The House gives the task of talking about the bill to a group of members. If the group has a good view of the bill, they give advice to the rest of the members how to vote for it. Next, the whole House convenes to talk about the bill. People who like the bill defend it. They try to convince everyone that it is good. They also often adjust the bill. This is because a lot of people don't like it. The House then votes on the bill. If there is a majority, it goes to the Senate.

Next, the senators have their chance to contemplate the bill. They talk about it. They put more emphasis on how the bill will change people's lives. They vote on it as well. If there is a majority, the bill goes to the president.

Finally, the president contemplates the bill. The president has two options. If he doesn't like it, he can veto it. A veto is when he doesn't sign it. If he likes it, he can sign the bill. This gives us a new law.

Lecture 3

W: OK, today we are going to talk about home remedies for illnesses.
M: What's a home remedy?
W: Glad you asked that. A home remedy is like medicine you can make at home. It makes you feel better when you are sick. Home remedies usually aren't very sophisticated. They are usually straightforward and require minimal effort. Unfortunately, they are not all considered legitimate by doctors. Are there any questions? No? Great, let's get started.

How many of you have ever had a black eye? It can hurt and be very embarrassing. Some doctors give the advice to put a cold can of soda on your cheek. This will keep your eye from getting too big.

How about sunburn—anyone ever had that? This is what happens when you stay outside in the sun too long. Your skin turns red and hurts really badly. If this happens, put potato or cucumber slices on the burnt area. This will make your skin feel much better.

How many of your fathers or mothers snore? This is when you make a loud sound with your nose when you sleep. If this happens, tell your parents to adjust their diet. Tell them to exercise. Losing weight is an easy way to stop snoring.

Finally, we have all had colds. It is hard to get them to go away. But if we all drink plenty of orange and lemon juice, they will go away much quicker. Oranges have a lot of vitamin C. This helps the body to fight the sickness.

Now, maybe some of you are not yet convinced of these remedies. That's OK. But next time you feel sick or hurt, try these. They're cheap and easy. Who knows? It might make you feel better.

Conversation 2

W: Hi, can I help you?
M: Yeah, can you give me some information about studying abroad next term.
W: Unfortunately, the deadline to sign up has already passed.
M: Aww . . . [*Disappointed.*] I wasn't aware of the deadline.
W: I can help you to sign up for the following term.
M: Well, I suppose I'll have to do that. I really want to do an exchange program. I suppose missing the deadline was my error anyway. What's the first thing that I have to do?
W: Well, do you know where you want to study?
M: Not really. I was thinking about Europe.
W: OK, well here is a list of schools in Europe that we have an exchange partnership with.
M: What if I want to go somewhere that isn't on the list?
W: Well, we can switch you to another program with another university. If you decide to do this, you must let us know early. This is so we can talk to the other university's administration to get everything set up.
M: OK, great. Do you have any advice on where I should study?
W: Well, the majority of the students who study in Europe really enjoy going to Spain. If it were me, though, I would go to China.
M: China? Really? Why?
W: It is really interesting and is a great place to be now.
M: Hmmm . . . I hadn't thought about that. I'll go home and look this over. Thanks for your help.

Answer Key

[Unit 1]

Conversation

Pages 18–19

A

1. A   2. B

B

Man - Student	Woman - Student Guide
• Can't find <u>the student center</u> • <u>Asks what's in the student center</u> • <u>Thinks it sounds like a good place to hang out</u>	• It is next to the <u>auditorium. It is a great place to hang out</u> • The bookstore, cafeteria, <u>and the recreation and newspaper office are there</u> • You can buy <u>concert tickets and get a discount</u> • <u>Need to take student ID</u>

C

1. B   2. B   3. A

D

1. assistance   2. verify   3. recreation
4. discount   5. collect

Page 20

Man - University Employee	Woman - Student
• The tickets are different <u>prices</u> • <u>Students that go to the university get a discount</u> • Students ticket $10, <u>non-student $15</u> • <u>Collect them at the auditorium</u> • <u>Next to the recreation office</u> • <u>Starts at 7 p.m.</u> • <u>Take ID to verify the name</u>	• Wants to buy tickets for <u>tonight's jazz concert</u> • Would like to buy one ticket for <u>herself and one for a friend</u> • <u>Still wants tickets</u>

1. A   2. C   3. C   4. B

Lecture

Pages 22–23

A

1. B   2. B   3. A   4. B

B and C

Underlined answers are from part B.

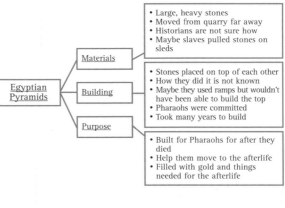

D

1. A   2. B   3. A

E

1. Furthermore   2. committed   3. structure
4. historians   5. ancient

Pages 24–25

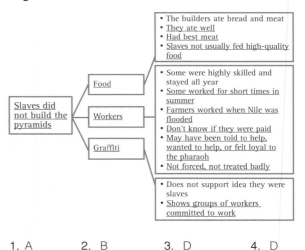

1. A   2. B   3. D   4. D
5. D   6. Yes, Yes, No, No

Check-up

Page 26

A

1. B   2. D

B

1. afterlife   2. student center   3. hang out
4. quarry   5. pyramids   6. auditorium
7. pharaoh   8. supplies

[Unit 2]

Conversation

Pages 28–29

A

1. B   2. A

B

Woman - Student	Man - RA
• Needs help with <u>accommodation bill</u> • Thinks she should be due <u>a refund</u> • <u>Is positive it's a mistake</u> • <u>Has receipt</u> • <u>Going to take care of it right now</u>	• Directs her to Office of <u>Accommodation; they should be able to help</u> • Tells her to take <u>care of this so it's not a burden</u> • <u>Office should be open for another hour</u>

C

1. B   2. B   3. B

D

1. accommodation   2. presume   3. Apparently
4. orientation   5. burden

Page 30

Man - Student	Woman - RA
• Moving out <u>of the dorm</u> • <u>3 roommates a burden</u> • <u>Moving in with brother, 3 blocks from school</u> • <u>Plans to move on Friday</u>	• Heard he is <u>moving out</u> • Might receive <u>partial refund, full refund if decision made within 3 weeks of orientation</u> • <u>Collect refund from Accommodation Office</u>

1. A   2. B   3. B   4. B

Lecture

Pages 32–33

A

1. B   2. A   3. A   4. B

B and C

Underlined answers are from part B.

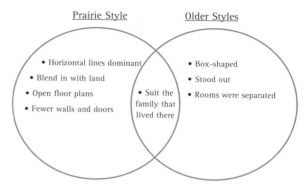

Architectural Styles

Prairie Style   Older Styles

Prairie Style:
• Horizontal lines dominant
• Blend in with land
• Open floor plans
• Fewer walls and doors

Overlap:
• Suit the family that lived there

Older Styles:
• Box-shaped
• Stood out
• Rooms were separated

D

1. B   2. B   3. B

E

1. horizontal   2. several   3. carve
4. architectural   5. contrary

Pages 34–35

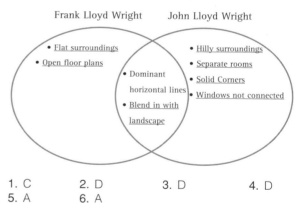

Architectural Styles

Frank Lloyd Wright   John Lloyd Wright

Frank Lloyd Wright:
• Flat surroundings
• Open floor plans

Overlap:
• Dominant horizontal lines
• Blend in with landscape

John Lloyd Wright:
• Hilly surroundings
• Separate rooms
• Solid Corners
• Windows not connected

1. C   2. D   3. D   4. D
5. A   6. A

Check-up

Page 36

A

1. C   2. A

B

1. dominant   2. payment   3. prairies
4. RA   5. stand out   6. mistakes
7. floor plan 8. refunded

Answer Key

[Unit 3]

Conversation

Pages 38–39

A
1. A   2. A

B

Man - Student	Woman - Professor
• Would like to speak about his application for the business studies graduate program • Has first draft of it • Would like the professor to look at it and give advice on how to improve it • Has been studying very hard all term • Will do his best in his exams	• The deadline for applications is next week • On the first page, he should list his main skills • A good way to proceed after the opening statement • Has marked down a few spelling mistakes • Looks like a good application

C
1. A   2. B   3. A

D
1. draft   2. graduate   3. submit
4. proceed   5. candidates

Page 40

Woman - Student	Man - Professor
• Heard that the professor was looking for a student to help with research • Was wondering if he had picked anyone yet • Has submitted an application • Thinks that she would be great for the job • Is studying in the chemistry graduate program	• Needs help with the research on the paper he is working on • It is unpaid but get a better grade and good experience • Hasn't made any decisions yet, a lot of students applied • Believes the student is very interested • The deadline for the paper is at the end of the year at exam time • Will proceed with interviews and choose soon

1. B   2. A   3. D
4. False, True, False, True

Lecture

Pages 42–43

A
1. B   2. A   3. B   4. C

B and C
Underlined answers are from part B.

Problem	Solution
Plant Diseases • Biological problem • Hard to get rid of • Spread by germs	→ Prevent the diseases • Use clean soil • Water plants well • Check plants • Pull out diseased plants
Farmers often grow one kind of crop and disease spreads easily	→ • Keep plants healthy • Plant different crops each year • If plants get really sick, use poison

D
1. B   2. A   3. B

E
1. produce   2. ecosystem   3. disease
4. biological 5. organisms

Pages 44–45

Problem	Solution
Insects damage plants • They eat plants • They make their nests and lay eggs inside plants • They carry disease • They cause a lot of damage • Farmers can lose a lot of money	→ Check plants daily • Take insects off plants • Pull out dead plants/leaves • Keep new plants away from others for one month • If a lot of insects, use poison but it can hurt the plants and is not good for the environment

1. C   2. C   3. C   4. A
5. D   6. A and C

Check-up

Page 46

A
1. A   2. D

B
1. program   2. crops   3. Maize
4. application   5. statement   6. poison
7. deadline   8. human

[Unit 4]

Conversation

Pages 48–49

A

1. B   2. A

B

Man - Student	Woman - Head of Canteen
• Would like to complain about <u>the canteen menu</u> • <u>Has a wheat allergy</u> • <u>Can only eat baked potatoes and fruit at the canteen</u> • <u>Would like more food made without bread or flour in it</u> • <u>Has a lot of good recipes for food without wheat in it</u>	• Would like the student to <u>elaborate</u> • The canteen does have <u>some food with no wheat in it</u> • Has a commitment to <u>make food that everyone can eat</u> • <u>Under pressure to make food that everyone likes</u> • <u>Will do her best to help</u> • <u>Difficult to keep everyone happy</u>

C

1. B   2. B   3. B

D

1. inspiration   2. pressure   3. elaborate
4. occasion   5. commitment

Page 50

Woman - Student	Man - Canteen Employee
• Is a <u>vegan</u> • Is wondering what <u>food she can eat today</u> • Will not eat <u>anything that comes from an animal</u> • <u>Not an allergy</u> • <u>Sometimes cannot eat anything from the canteen</u> • <u>Would like more food with vegetables and rice</u> • <u>Today will have the baked potato and salad</u>	• Thinks a vegan is like <u>a vegetarian</u> • On today's menu, there are <u>baked potatoes or the salad bar</u> • <u>Thinks it must take real commitment to be a vegan</u> • <u>It must be difficult sometimes</u> • <u>Will ask the chef if he can make more vegan food</u>

1. B   2. C   3. B   4. D

Lecture

Pages 52–53

A

1. B   2. B   3. B   4. A

B and C

Underlined answers are from part B.

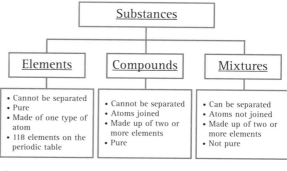

D

1. B   2. A   3. B

E

1. compound   2. periodic table   3. Despite
4. element   5. mixture

Pages 54–55

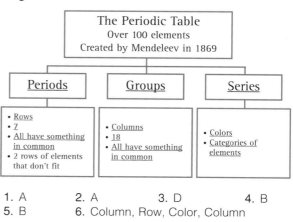

1. A   2. A   3. D   4. B
5. B   6. Column, Row, Color, Column

Check-up

Page 56

A

1. B   2. B

B

1. atoms   2. complaint   3. pure   4. join
5. allergy   6. served   7. type   8. canteen

Answer Key

[Unit 5]

Conversation

Pages 58–59

A
1. B   2. A

B

Woman - Student	Man - University Employee
• Needs to pay a <u>parking ticket</u> • <u>Was parked by library</u> • Has hurt leg and <u>didn't know she needed a permit</u> • Received ticket for <u>parking in a permit specific area</u> • <u>Is glad it is not a ticket</u> • <u>Would be good to bring car to school</u>	• Need a permit to <u>park anywhere on campus</u> • It isn't a ticket; it is a <u>warning</u> • <u>Urges student to get a permit</u> • <u>With permit, you can park almost anywhere</u> • <u>Get permit from security office</u> • <u>Need driver's license</u> • With note from doctor, can get handicapped permit <u>and park close to buildings</u> • <u>Security office is next door</u>

C
1. B   2. A   3. B

D
1. security   2. urge   3. license
4. Subsequent   5. violation

Page 60

Man - Student	Woman - University Employee
• Needs to purchase <u>a handicap-parking permit</u> • Got a warning from <u>security</u> • <u>Also brought a note from doctor</u> • <u>Asks if there is anywhere he shouldn't park</u>	• Needs driver's <u>license and license plate number</u> • <u>Hang permit in rear-view mirror</u> • <u>Permit must be seen</u> • <u>Check signs as to where to park</u> • <u>Any more violations means getting a ticket</u>

1. B   2. C   3. A   4. C

Lecture

Pages 62–63

A
1. A   2. B   3. B   4. C

B and C
Underlined answers are from part B.

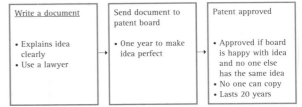
Patents - To Protect an Idea

D
1. B   2. A   3. A

E
1. document   2. procedure   3. complex
4. seek   5. approve

Pages 64–65

Starting a Business

Get a patent	Get money	Get a place	Get workers
• <u>Stop rivals stealing idea</u> • Ask a lawyer to help	• To buy things • <u>To pay workers</u> • <u>Borrow from bank</u> • Pay back quickly	• <u>Work from home (cheap)</u> • If business grows, get a factory	• <u>Hard-working</u> • People you can trust

1. A   2. B   3. D   4. B
5. A   6. C

Check-up

Page 66

A
1. C   2. B

B
1. permits   2. patents   3. warning
4. board   5. retail   6. ticket
7. rivals   8. handicap

[Unit 6]

Conversation

Pages 68–69

A

1. B   2. A

B

Woman - Student	Man - Professor
• Project due today but <u>wasn't able to turn it in</u> • Computer <u>crashed and lost all her work</u> • <u>Wondering if she could have extension</u> • Could re-write and <u>give him it at the end of next week</u> • <u>Will finish over weekend</u>	• Understands, but <u>is unacceptable that she waited until last day to finish project</u> • Can't give <u>a weeks extension</u> • <u>It is important to backup all work</u> • <u>Will give a couple of extra days</u> • <u>Only going to give half credit</u>

C

1. A   2. A   3. B

D

1. credit   2. Nonetheless
3. unacceptable   4. marking
5. time consuming

Page 70

Woman - Professor	Man - Student
• Noticed essay was <u>not turned in</u> • Irresponsibility is <u>unacceptable</u> • <u>Only going to give half credit</u>	• Needs an <u>extension</u> • <u>Can't seem to keep up with other class work</u> • <u>Has draft, but didn't bring it</u>

1. C   2. D   3. B   4. A

Lecture

Pages 72–73

A

1. A   2. B   3. A   4. C

B and C

Underlined answers are from part B.

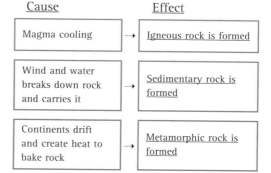

The Rock Cycle

Cause		Effect
Magma cooling	→	<u>Igneous rock is formed</u>
Wind and water breaks down rock and carries it	→	<u>Sedimentary rock is formed</u>
Continents drift and create heat to bake rock	→	<u>Metamorphic rock is formed</u>

D

1. B   2. A   3. B

E

1. illustrate   2. cycle   3. drift   4. crystal
5. constantly

Pages 74–75

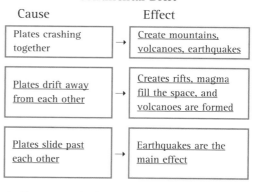

Continental Drift

Cause		Effect
Plates crashing together	→	<u>Create mountains, volcanoes, earthquakes</u>
Plates drift away from each other	→	<u>Creates rifts, magma fill the space, and volcanoes are formed</u>
Plates slide past each other	→	<u>Earthquakes are the main effect</u>

1. D   2. A   3. D   4. B
5. B   6. Yes, Yes, No, Yes

Check-up

Page 76

A

1. B   2. D

B

1. backup   2. disk   3. Sedimentary
4. rewrite   5. Magma   6. Igneous
7. Metamorphic 8. computer crash

Answer Key

[Review 1]

Conversation 1

Page 77

Woman - Student	Man - Professor
• She is applying to <u>grad school</u> • She thinks she did well <u>on her GRE's</u> • <u>She asks him for a letter of recommendation</u> • <u>Her application deadline is February</u> • <u>She has already arranged to have her transcripts sent to the schools</u>	• He thinks she is a good <u>candidate for graduate studies</u> • <u>He will finish her letter of recommendation by Friday</u> • <u>He thinks seniors are under a lot of pressure</u>

1. A   2. D   3. A   4. B

Lecture 1

Pages 78–79

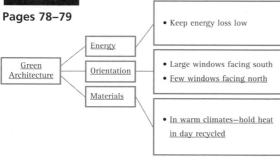

1. D   2. A   3. A   4. B
5. C   6. C

Lecture 2

Pages 80–81

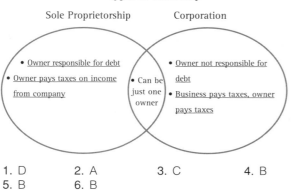

1. D   2. A   3. C   4. B
5. B   6. B

Lecture 3

Pages 82–83

Problem		Solution
Plants need energy	→	Get it from sunlight
Plants need water	→	Get it from soil via roots
Plants need nutrients	→	Get it from soil via roots
Plants need to reproduce	→	Pollination

1. A   2. A   3. B   4. A
5. D   6. D

Conversation 2

Page 84

Man - Student	Woman - Receptionist
• Seeking <u>employment</u> • Explains that he is on <u>scholarship</u> • <u>He needs money for accommodation</u> • <u>He applied for a loan but it wasn't approved</u> • <u>No experience but will apply</u> • <u>Will take security job</u>	• Tells him he's <u>late in applying for work</u> • <u>Tells him sometimes students drop out early—jobs become available</u> • <u>Finds an opening for a security job</u> • <u>Explains procedure for application</u>

1. B   2. B   3. B   4. A

[Unit 7]

Conversation

Pages 86–87

A
1. A   2. B

B

Woman - Student	Man - University Employee
• Needs to <u>pay for classes</u> • Wondering if there is open <u>enrollment in art history</u> • <u>Would like to register</u> • <u>Class was canceled last year so had to switch classes</u> • <u>Is a full-time student</u>	• Asks if student is registered in <u>all the courses she want to take</u> • Half of the tuition is <u>due now, half the first day</u> • <u>Best to pay at administration office</u> • <u>Explains refund will be given if she drops the class within first two weeks</u>

C
1. B   2. A   3. A

D
1. administration   2. register   3. guarantee
4. open enrollment 5. enroll

Page 88

Woman - University Employee	Man - Student
• Asks the reason for <u>dropping the class</u> • <u>Thinks it's two days past deadline</u> • <u>Has until today to drop a class</u> • <u>Tells student to enroll in less time-consuming class</u> • <u>The student won't receive a refund</u>	• Class is not what he <u>expected</u> • Wants to receive a <u>refund</u> • Spoke to Derrick at <u>the administration office</u> • <u>He wants to remain as a full-time student and enroll in weight training</u>

1. C   2. A   3. B   4. C

Lecture

Pages 90–91

A
1. B   2. A   3. A   4. C

B and C
Underlined answers are from part B.

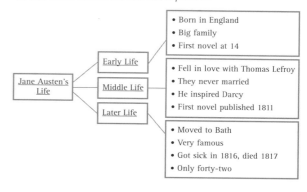

D
1. B   2. B   3. No, Yes, No, Yes

E
1. intelligent   2. reveal   3. request
4. sophisticated   5. general

Pages 92–93

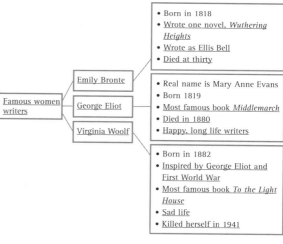

1. C   2. A   3. B   4. C
5. B   6. YES, YES, NO, NO

Check-up

Page 94

A
1. A   2. B

B
1. apologize   2. humor   3. siblings
4. full-time   5. expect   6. biographies
7. drop a class 8. switch

Answer Key

[Unit 8]

Conversation

Pages 96–97

A

1. B   2. A

B

Man - Student	Woman - University Employee
• About to finish the first year of <u>a history degree</u> • Is considering studying <u>abroad for a semester</u> • <u>Would really like to study in France</u> • <u>Has some family in France</u> • <u>Speaks a little French</u>	• Has a few <u>options</u> • University has partnerships and <u>exchange programs with schools all over the world</u> • <u>Has exchange program in Paris</u> • <u>Knowing the language will help him settle in</u> • <u>Will forward the information to him tomorrow</u>

C

1. B   2. A   3. A

D

1. option   2. immigration   3. abroad
4. exchange   5. partnership

Page 98

Woman - Student	Man - University Employee
• Is a student from <u>Mexico</u> • Arrived last semester and <u>is having a few problems</u> • Is an <u>exchange student</u> • <u>This university and hers have a partnership</u> • <u>Will be here a year</u> • <u>Is struggling with the language</u> • <u>Wants the tutor</u> • <u>Also needs to fill out a form for immigration</u>	• Is here to help <u>students from abroad with any issues they have</u> • <u>There are a couple of options</u> • Can change classes <u>to make them easier for her</u> • <u>Can provide a student tutor</u> • <u>Will forward the forms to the student</u>

1. A   2. D   3. C   4. A

Lecture

Pages 100–101

A

1. A   2. A   3. B   4. B

B and C

Underlined answers are from part B.

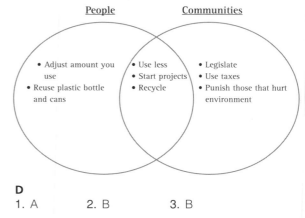

D

1. A   2. B   3. B

E

1. legislate   2. adjust   3. aware
4. globe   5. initiate

Pages 102–103

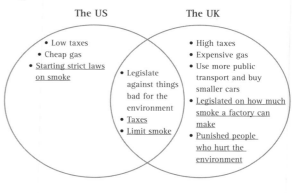

1. D   2. C   3. B   4. A
5. B   6. C

Check-up

Page 104

A

1. B   2. C

B

1. forward   2. issues   3. fair
4. settle in   5. strict   6. passes
7. details   8. reuse

[Unit 9]

Conversation

Pages 106–107

A

1. B   2. A

B

Man - Student	Woman - Professor
• Invited to <u>enter an essay competition for students</u> • Is not sure what <u>to write about</u> • Must write about something that he likes and <u>his interpretation of it</u> • <u>Agrees that the best option might be to write about one of his favorite books</u> • <u>Is worried he might not do a good job</u>	• Congratulates <u>the student on being invited to enter</u> • A number of teachers have <u>praised his writing work</u> • <u>Thinks the student should write about his favorite book</u> • <u>He should give lots of reasons and examples</u> • <u>Should convince people that he has really thought about the book</u>

C

1. B   2. A   3. B

D

1. interpretation   2. advice   3. convince
4. ambition   5. contemplate

Pages 108

Woman - Student	Man - Professor
• Has been asked to show <u>her work at a university art show</u> • It has been an <u>ambition of hers</u> • <u>Feels nervous</u> • <u>Is her first show</u> • Has had a lot of praise from <u>her teachers</u> • <u>Is contemplating the reaction of others</u> • <u>Teachers and professionals will review her art</u> • <u>Will enjoy the good reviews and forget the bad ones</u>	• Has seen <u>her art work</u> • Is convinced <u>that everybody will love it</u> • <u>It will be a new experience</u> • Everybody's interpretation of art is different • <u>You cannot control what people see in your work</u>

1. C   2. B   3. C   4. D

Lecture

Pages 110–111

A

1. A   2. B   3. A   4. C

B and C

Underlined answers are from part B.

Problem	Solution
Want to study better →	Make small changes to help your brain
• Hard to concentrate on work →	• Get more sleep
• Feel lazy and unhealthy →	• Change your diet
• Difficult to start work →	• Go to the gym and exercise

D

1. B   2. D   3. B

E

1. minimal   2. output   3. excluded
4. implementation   5. equates

Pages 112–113

Problem	Solution
Feel bad →	<u>Have a balanced lifestyle</u>
• Friend plays computers all day, doesn't want <u>to be friends anymore</u> →	• <u>Make time for friends and games</u>
• Good student, always studies, but <u>always sick</u> →	• <u>Do other things, like going to the gym and having fun will make him feel better</u>
• Workers were not happy, didn't <u>have good output</u> →	• <u>Spend time with family, have a balanced lifestyle.</u>

1. C   2. D   3. B   4. A
5. D   6. A

Check-up

Page 114

A

1. C   2. B

B

1. praise   2. gym   3. review
4. alert   5. a number of   6. quantities
7. symptom   8. congratulations

Answer Key

[Unit 10]

Conversation

Pages 116–117

A
1. A   2. A

B

Man - Student	Woman - University Employee
• Has lost <u>his student identification card</u> • Cannot remember <u>his student number</u> • <u>Is a new undergraduate</u> • <u>Doesn't think the card was stolen. He misplaced it</u> • <u>Has not had a lot of luck with his student cards</u>	• Needs the student's <u>name and identification number</u> • Lots of students lose <u>their ID cards</u> • Details indicate that <u>the student has lost two ID cards in one month</u> • <u>Student should be more careful in future</u> • <u>Will have to pay a fee for his replacement card</u>

C
1. A   2. B   3. A

D
1. term   2. database   3. undergraduate
4. declares   5. indicate

Page 118

Woman - Student	Man - University Employee
• Is a <u>third year nursing undergraduate</u> • Would like a <u>replacement student ID card</u> • Still has <u>her old student card</u> • <u>Old student card is two years old</u> • <u>The picture on it is old and she does not like it</u> • <u>She looks different from when the photograph was first taken</u> • <u>Only wants a new photograph on her card</u>	• Would like to know <u>why the student needs a new card</u> • Must declare <u>her old card lost, damaged, or stolen to get a new one</u> • Asks if there is <u>anything wrong with the current card</u> • <u>Sees nothing wrong with the current card</u> • <u>Once a photograph is put in the database, it cannot be changed</u> • <u>Cannot give new cards to students anytime they want</u>

1. D   2. B   3. A   4. A

Lecture

Pages 120–121

A
1. A   2. B   3. B   4. A

B and C
Underlined answers are from part B.

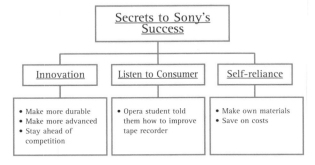

D
1. C   2. C   3. D

E
1. predominantly   2. commission   3. innovation
4. phase   5. competitive

Pages 122–123

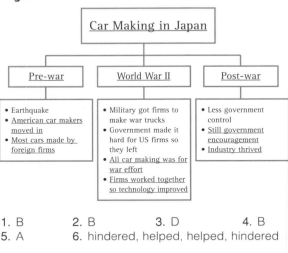

1. B   2. B   3. D   4. B
5. A   6. hindered, helped, helped, hindered

Check-up

Page 124

A
1. A   2. D

B
1. electronics   2. anytime   3. self-reliance
4. replacement   5. durable   6. careless
7. misplace   8. thrive

[Unit 11]

Conversation

Pages 126–127

A

1. A   2. B

B

Man - Student	Woman - University Employee
• Is having trouble with his laptop computer • Thinks that it may have a virus • Has a lot of assignments due and needs the information on his computer • Doesn't know what he will do if he loses his files • Cannot open any of his files • Has never had a virus before	• Can have a look at the computer for the student • Asks if the computer has an anti-virus program • It is a program that defends it from unwanted viruses • It is very important to have it on a computer • Can see a virus on the computer • Will install another anti-virus program on the computer • Student can pick up the computer later today

C

1. B   2. A   3. B

D

1. defend   2. tasks   3. resistant
4. file   5. assignment

Pages 128

Woman - Student	Man - University Employee
• Her laptop computer has stopped working • Dropped it and now it won't turn on • Has a big assignment to finish • Has a lot of important files on the computer • Would like the university worker to fix it	• Laptops are not too resistant to being dropped • A padded laptop bag is a good way to protect it • When the computer is on, the light on the battery comes on • Hopes that this means that the computer is all right • Thinks that the power button has broken • Normally, the IT center does not do that kind of repair • He will try to fix it for the student

1. C   2. C   3. A   4. D

Lecture

Pages 130–131

A

1. B   2. A   3. A   4. B

B and C

Underlined answers are from part B.

How to Become President

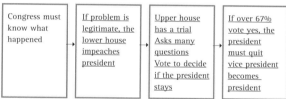

Declare they want to be president Must choose party	Election within each party Party decides whom it likes best	A big election Tell ideas to everyone	People decide on next president

D

1. A   2. B   3. A

E

1. distinguish   2. significant   3. convened
4. straightforward   5. legitimate

Pages 132–133

Impeachment

Congress must know what happened	If problem is legitimate, the lower house impeaches president	Upper house has a trial Asks many questions Vote to decide if the president stays	If over 67% vote yes, the president must quit vice president becomes president

1. B   2. A   3. A   4. C
5. A   6. D

Check-up

Page 134

A

1. C   2. D

B

1. states   2. laptop   3. IT
4. install   5. impeached   6. parties
7. elections   8. virus

Answer Key

[Unit 12]

Conversation

Pages 136–137

A
1. B   2. B

B

Man - Student	Woman - Professor
• Having problems getting <u>lab notes posted online</u> • Information is not being <u>transmitted</u> • <u>Receiving error message and blank page</u> • <u>He is thankful for help</u>	• Corresponds to students <u>using the course web site</u> • Asks if he has tried other <u>sites or if he has entered in the wrong web address</u> • <u>Instructs student to go try it out</u> • <u>Wants to know if it works</u>

C
1. A   2. B   3. B

D
1. errors   2. via   3. transmit
4. majority   5. correspond

Page 138

Woman - Student	Man - Professor
• Needs <u>lecture and lab notes</u> • Backpack <u>was stolen with everything in it</u> • <u>Save lots of time by not having to copy notes from someone else</u>	• Asks what the reason is • Posts all notes <u>online</u> • <u>Will give access to notes online</u> • <u>Sometimes the site has trouble transmitting</u> • <u>Just retype address to see site</u>

1. D   2. C   3. D   4. A

Lecture

Pages 140–141

A
1. B   2. B   3. B   4. C

B and C
Underlined answers are from part B.

A Good Presentation

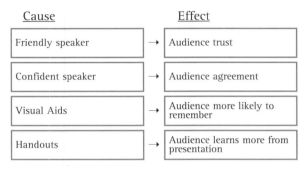

Cause		Effect
Friendly speaker	→	Audience trust
Confident speaker	→	Audience agreement
Visual Aids	→	Audience more likely to remember
Handouts	→	Audience learns more from presentation

D
1. A   2. A   3. B

E
1. comprised   2. resolution   3. emphasis
4. views   5. reluctant

Pages 142–143

Debating

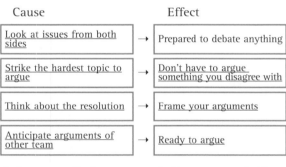

Cause		Effect
<u>Look at issues from both sides</u>	→	Prepared to debate anything
<u>Strike the hardest topic to argue</u>	→	<u>Don't have to argue something you disagree with</u>
<u>Think about the resolution</u>	→	<u>Frame your arguments</u>
<u>Anticipate arguments of other team</u>	→	<u>Ready to argue</u>

1. B   2. A   3. B   4. B
5. D   6. A

Check-up

Page 144

A
1. A   2. D

B
1. presentations   2. blank   3. Handouts
4. lab   5. visual aids 6. site
7. graph   8. post

[Review 2]

Conversation 1

Page 145

Woman - Student	Man - Professor
• Needs some <u>help</u> • Can't find anything that can <u>defend point of view</u> • <u>Didn't find anything at the library</u> • <u>Will get group and start research tonight</u>	• Needs to <u>go to class</u> • Can start by going to <u>library</u> • Can use <u>the database from government's commission on nature</u>. • <u>Significant amount of information</u> • <u>More importantly lots of information to help defend position</u> • <u>Will take a long time</u> • <u>Good parts will distinguish themselves easily</u>

1. B   2. A   3. D   4. B

Lecture 1

Pages 146–147

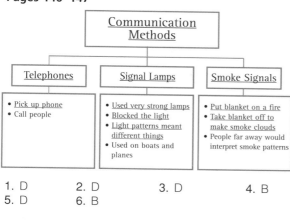

1. D   2. D   3. D   4. B
5. D   6. B

Lecture 2

Pages 148–149

Making Laws

The House	The Senate	The President
• <u>Writes a new bill</u> • <u>Gives task of talking about bill to members</u> • <u>Whole house convenes to talk about bill</u> • <u>House votes on bill</u> • Majority votes yes, bill goes to Senate	• <u>Contemplates bill</u> • <u>Talk about it</u> • <u>Ask how it will change lives</u> • <u>Vote</u> • If a majority, then goes to president	• <u>Contemplates bill</u> • <u>If he or she likes it, he can sign it</u> • If he or she doesn't like it, he or she can veto it

1. B   2. A   3. C   4. D
5. B   6. C

Lecture 3

Pages 150–151

Cause		Effect
Put cold soda can on cheek	→	Helps keep black eye from getting too big
Put potato and cucumber slices on burnt area	→	Helps skin feel better after sunburn
Lose weight and exercise	→	Helps people stop snoring when they sleep
Drink lots of orange and lemon juice	→	Can make colds go away much quicker.

1. B   2. D   3. A   4. A
5. C   6. D

Conversation 2

Page 152

Man - Student	Woman - Administrator
• Wants information about <u>studying abroad</u> • Missing the deadline was <u>his own fault</u> • Thinking about <u>Europe</u> • <u>Wants advice on where he should study</u> • <u>Will go home and look things over</u>	• Says that deadline <u>has passed</u> • Can help <u>sign up for next term</u> • Gives the student <u>a list of schools that have an exchange program with university</u> • <u>If student wants to go to another program, he must let them know early</u> • <u>Says majority enjoy Spain</u> • <u>Recommends going to China</u>

1. C   2. B   3. C   4. A